Raising the Torch!

A Salute to Birmingham's Southern Cuisine

Jefferson County Medical Society Alliance

Raising the Torch!
A Salute to Birmingham's Southern Cuisine

Published by the Jefferson County Medical Society Alliance
Copyright © 2006
Jefferson County Medical Society Alliance
901 South 18th Street
Birmingham, Alabama 35205
205-933-8601

PHOTOGRAPHS:
Birmingham Magazine—Skyline photo
Laynee McWilliams—Vulcan painting on front cover
Vulcan Park Foundation—Vulcan sketch
Birmingham Botanical Gardens—Red bridge photo
Jeannie Davis—additional photos

Edited, Designed, and Manufactured by

CommunityClassics™

An imprint of

P.O. Box 305142
Nashville, Tennessee 37230
800-358-0560
Manufactured in China
First Printing: 2006
3,000 copies

Dedication

At the heart of every gathering with family or friends is the

enjoyment of good cooking. As we dedicate this Alliance

cookbook to our physicians' spouses, we hope our recipes add

good times and good health to all of your special gatherings.

Special Acknowledgments

SPECIAL THANKS TO:

Birmingham Magazine for their exquisite skyline photo

Laynee McWilliams, artist, for her whimsical
Vulcan painting on our cover

Vulcan Park Foundation for the Vulcan sketch used as our icon

Birmingham Botanical Gardens for the use
of their beautiful red bridge for one of our photos

Jeannie Davis, photographer and one of our
members, whose photos are throughout our book

Jefferson County Medical Society Alliance Cookbook Committee

Chairman – Pam G. Cezayirli

Co-Chairman – Carole Thomas

Ginny Catalano

Millie Christopher

Sue Cylbulsky

Susan Dasher

Jeannie Davis

Angie Denton

Rosine Feist

Donna Huggins

Dianne Luketic

Cheré Prados

Winyss Shepard

Cyndy Uncapher

Dolly Walker

Nell Williams

Cindy Yielding

Jefferson County Medical Society Alliance Contributors List

Amy Albert
Melissa Aprahamian
Diane Baker
Kay Blankenship
Dr. Ben Branscomb
Ginny Catalano
Pam G. Cezayirli
Dr. Craig Christopher
Millie Christopher
Dr. Richard Cybulsky
Sue Cybulsky
Susan Dasher
Jeannie Davis
Dr. Jim Davis
Phyllis Deinlein
Dr. Ann Denton
Dr. Carter Denton
Janet Faught
Rosine Feist
Diane Fitzgerald
Donna Francavilla
Sherron Goldstein
Sheryl Gould
Ann Grotting
Carmen Habeeb
Dr. Hugh Hood
Susan Hudson
Donna Huggins
Susie T. Jander
Jenelle Jones
Patricia Johnson
Anne Lamkin
Mary Wills LeCroy
Debbie Lewis
Nicole Liechty

Dianne Luketic
D'Anne McCoy
Janet McPherson
Dr. Michael Moore
Stephanie Moore
Vina Morros
Susan Murphy
Marie Neighbors
Lynne Nicholson
Karen Nielsen
Holly O'Mara
Nelda Osment
Susan Padove
Gayle Palmer
Billie Pigford
Dr. Malcolm Pigford
Cheré Prados
Dot Renneker
Becky Rollins
Pat Scofield
Zena Schulman
Amy Scofield
Vicki Scofield
Winyss Shepard
Alice Slappey
Nancy Stetler
Ellen Staner
Carole Thomas
Cyndy Uncapher
Debbie Veren
Dolly Walker
Dr. Jim Walker
Frances Wideman
Nell Williams
Cindy Yeilding

Table of Contents

History of the Jefferson County Medical Society Alliance

The Jefferson County Medical Society Alliance was first organized as the Woman's Auxiliary to the Jefferson County Medical Society in 1923. The organizer and first president was Mrs. Seale Harris, a dynamic physician's spouse from this county who also helped organize and run state, national, and regional medical auxiliaries. The original purpose of the Auxiliary was to support the medical profession by promoting fellowship and understanding among physicians' families and by improving the health of the community.

By 1929, regular meetings were held and a loan fund was established to benefit a medical student from the county. Money was raised from benefit bridge parties and forty-cent lunches. A Loving Cup was awarded to the Jefferson County school with the best health program. The first yearbook was printed in 1933.

During the early 1940s, projects were focused on helping the war effort. After World War II, when the University of Alabama Medical School was established in Birmingham, the Auxiliary furnished a dayroom for women medical students, and later helped organize a Medical Students' Auxiliary. Throughout the 1950s and 60s it continued to gear its health projects to the changing needs of the community, spreading health information to schools and providing volunteers for such programs as the Sabin Oral Sundays (immunizing children against polio) and Diabetic Detection drives.

Fund-raising efforts intensified in the 1960s, 70s, and 80s in order to support both the American Medical Association Education and Research Foundation (AMA-ERF) and the Auxiliary's own local scholarships, which at that time went to student nurses and medical technicians. The Auxiliary has also continually contributed to a number of worthwhile health-related community projects. These included promoting health fairs and workshops, providing

dummies for CPR classes, creating a food fund for the Ronald McDonald House, infant car seat loaner programs through Children's Hospital, blood-donor drives, and a number of other projects. Its fund-raising efforts to support these projects have varied from the popular "Medical Musicals" of the 60s, to the sale of "optics" (hand-painted recycled eyeglass lenses used as jewelry) in the 70s, to the Kitchen Tours of the mid-80s to mid-90s. A Christmas "sharing card" was created to support AMA-ERF, annual auctions were held, and in the 1980s the first cookbook was published.

The organization incorporated in 1975 and dropped "Woman's" from its title, becoming the Jefferson County Medical Auxiliary so that male spouses of female physicians could join. The organization has also been involved in promoting good health legislation, especially since the 1960s. It has educated its own members on medical-related matters through speakers at its monthly meetings, and many of its members have risen to positions of leadership at the state and national level.

In the late 1980s, the Auxiliary began what is still one of its most successful programs, putting on a puppet show aimed at the prevention of child abuse, "Someone to Talk To." Third graders in public schools throughout the county see the show, in rotation. In the 1990s, working with Blue Cross Blue Shield of Alabama, the Children's Hospital, and the County Medical Society, the Auxiliary took the lead in creating Body Trek, a mobile health education classroom. The Auxiliary, by then the Alliance, also helped staff this interactive health museum on its visits to various county schools for several years, and won national recognition for the project. In 1999, Body Trek was turned over to Children's Hospital and Blue Cross Blue Shield. In the meantime, to raise the large sums required for the Body Trek project, the Alliance sponsored an annual golf tournament.

The Alliance encourages the spouses of all county physicians to join in its efforts to promote the good health of the community and the best interests of medicine. The sales from this Alliance cookbook will benefit our county, state, and national health projects for many years to come.

Mission Statement

The Jefferson County Medical Society Alliance is an organization

of physicians' spouses dedicated to promoting better health,

ensuring sound health legislation, funding medical education,

and providing support for the medical family.

Appetizers & Beverages

"You can grow old & ugly, but if you are a good cook the world will still beat a path to your door."

James Beard

Smoked Salmon Canapés

8 ounces cream cheese, softened
2 teaspoons lemon juice
1 teaspoon grated onion
Pinch of pepper
1 teaspoon dill weed (optional)

4 (7-inch) flour tortillas
1 tablespoon plus 1 teaspoon capers
8 ounces smoked salmon,
  thinly sliced
Sprigs of fresh dill (optional)

Mix the cream cheese, lemon juice, onion, pepper and dill weed in a bowl. Spread evenly over the tortillas. Sprinkle with the capers. Layer the salmon over the capers. Roll up the tortillas. Chill until serving time. Cut each roll into 6 slices. Top each piece with a sprig of fresh dill.

Makes 24 servings

Tomato Phyllo Pizza

1 (1-pound) package phyllo dough
1 cup (2 sticks) butter, melted
  and clarified
1/2 cup each (2 ounces each)
  grated Parmesan cheese and
  Romano cheese
2 onions, thinly sliced

5 tomatoes, thinly sliced
8 ounces feta cheese, crumbled
1/4 cup chopped fresh thyme
3 tablespoons fresh oregano
7 sprigs fresh basil, chopped
  (optional)
Sprigs of thyme

Layer 4 sheets of the phyllo dough on a buttered 11x14-inch baking sheet with a raised edge, brushing each sheet with the melted butter. Continue layering at least 8 more sheets of the phyllo dough, brushing each sheet with melted butter and sprinkling with a little Parmesan cheese and Romano cheese. Layer the onions, tomatoes, feta cheese, 1/4 cup thyme, the oregano and basil over the top sheet of phyllo. Bake at 350 degrees for 20 minutes or until golden brown. Garnish with sprigs of thyme.

Makes 10 to 12 servings

Note: This "pizza" makes a wonderful meatless entrée as well. Just slice into larger pieces and serve with a tossed salad and crisp white wine. The recipe is a variation of one published in *Gourmet*, August 1989.

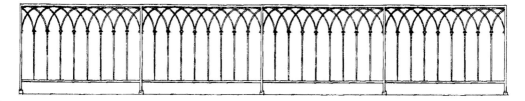

Miniature Shrimp Quiches

The pastry shells:
1/2 cup (1 stick) butter, softened
4 ounces cream cheese, softened
1 1/2 cups all-purpose flour
1/4 teaspoon salt

The shrimp filling:
1 cup (4 ounces) shredded Swiss cheese
1/2 cup finely chopped cooked shrimp
2 tablespoons chopped fresh chives
1/2 teaspoon thyme
2 eggs
1/2 cup half-and-half
1/4 teaspoon salt
1/4 teaspoon pepper
1/4 teaspoon nutmeg
Dash of hot red pepper sauce

For the pastry shells, beat the butter and cream cheese in a mixing bowl at medium speed until fluffy. Stir in the flour and salt. Chill, covered, for 1 hour. Shape into 1-inch balls. Press over the bottom and up the side of 36 ungreased miniature muffin cups.

For the shrimp filling, combine the cheese, shrimp, chives and thyme in a bowl and mix well. Spoon into the pastry shells. Combine the eggs, half-and-half, salt, pepper, nutmeg and hot sauce in a bowl and mix well. Spoon evenly into the pastry shells. Bake at 350 degrees for 30 to 35 minutes or until set.

Makes 18 servings

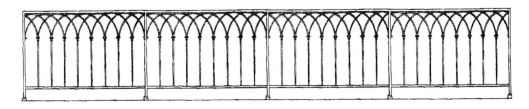

Spinach and Bacon Quiche

2 cups packed chopped fresh baby spinach
1 pound bacon, crisp-cooked and crumbled
1 1/2 cups (6 ounces) shredded Swiss cheese
1 unbaked (9-inch) pie shell
6 eggs, beaten
1 1/2 cups heavy cream or whipping cream
Salt and pepper to taste

Layer the spinach, bacon and cheese in the pie shell. Process the eggs, cream, salt and pepper in a food processor or blender. Pour into the pie shell. Bake at 375 degrees for 35 to 45 minutes or until set. Cut into 8 wedges.

Makes 8 servings

Variations: Sauté some chopped onion and sliced mushrooms in the bacon drippings and add to the quiche filling. Sprinkle the quiche with a little nutmeg before baking. Or substitute chopped green onions for the spinach and add 1/2 cup (2 ounces) grated Parmesan cheese.

"Cooking is like love. It should be entered into with abandon or not at all."
—*Harriet Van Horne*

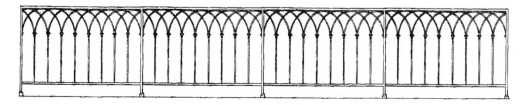

Dill Cucumber on Party Bread

3 ounces cream cheese, softened
1 tablespoon mayonnaise
1 envelope Italian salad dressing mix
1 loaf party-size rye or pumpernickel bread, sliced
2 cucumbers, thinly sliced
Dill weed

Combine the cream cheese, mayonnaise and salad dressing mix in a bowl and mix well. Spread on the bread slices. Top with the cucumber slices and sprinkle lightly with dill weed.

Makes 8 to 10 servings

Cucumber Sandwiches

1 (8-count) can refrigerator crescent rolls, or
　1 loaf frozen bread dough, thawed
12 ounces cream cheese, softened
1 envelope Italian salad dressing mix
3 cucumbers, peeled and thinly sliced

For the crescent rolls, unroll the dough. Press the perforations to seal and cut with a cookie cutter into desired shapes or cut into 2-inch squares. Bake using the package directions. Cool on a wire rack.

For the bread dough, snip 2 inches from one end of the dough. Fit the dough into a bread mold coated with nonstick cooking spray. Bake with the mold standing on end at 375 degrees until golden brown. Remove from the mold. Cool on a wire rack. Cut into thin slices.

Combine the cream cheese and salad dressing mix in a bowl and mix well. Spread on the crescent roll pieces or thin slices of bread. Top with the cucumber slices.

Makes 12 servings

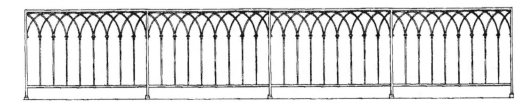

Garden Harvest Squares

2 (8-count) cans refrigerator
  crescent rolls
8 ounces cream cheese, softened
1/2 cup sour cream
1 teaspoon dill weed
1/4 teaspoon garlic powder
20 (or more) small broccoli florets
20 (or more) thin cucumber slices or
  zucchini slices

10 (or more) cherry
  tomatoes, sliced
Chopped green onions
1 (4-ounce) can chopped black
  olives (optional)
Chopped green, red or yellow bell
  peppers (optional)
Chopped fresh parsley

Unroll the crescent roll dough. Separate into 4 long rectangles. Arrange the strips crosswise in a 10×15-inch baking pan coated with nonstick cooking spray. Press over the bottom and up the sides to form a crust. Bake at 375 degrees for 13 to 17 minutes or until golden brown. Cool completely. Combine the cream cheese, sour cream, dill weed and garlic powder in a small bowl and mix well. Chill, covered, for 1 to 2 hours. Spread over the cooled crust. Cut into small squares. Top with the broccoli, cucumbers, tomatoes, green onions, olives, bell peppers and fresh parsley.

Makes 40 to 60 servings

Marinated Cheese

1 (8-ounce) block sharp Cheddar
  cheese, cut into squares
1 (8-ounce) block cream cheese,
  cut into squares
1/2 cup olive oil
1/2 cup white wine vinegar
1 (2-ounce) jar diced pimentos

3 garlic cloves, minced
3 tablespoons minced green onions
3 tablespoons chopped fresh
  parsley or cilantro
1 teaspoon sugar
1/2 teaspoon each salt and pepper
1/4 teaspoon basil

Form a block of alternating Cheddar cheese and cream cheese squares on a serving platter with sides. Combine the olive oil, vinegar, pimentos, garlic, green onions, parsley, sugar, salt, pepper and basil in a bowl and mix well. Pour over the cheese block. Marinate in the refrigerator for 8 hours.

Makes 15 to 20 servings

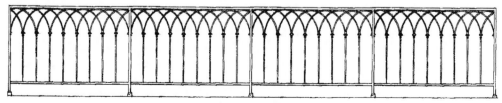

Crostini with Tomato Goat Cheese Spread

The crostini:
3 baguettes, cut diagonally into $1/4$-inch slices
$1/2$ cup extra-virgin olive oil
$1/2$ cup finely chopped fresh dill weed
Chopped fresh thyme and rosemary to taste
Minced garlic to taste

The tomato goat cheese spread:
2 (8-ounce) logs plain goat cheese, softened
$1/2$ cup drained oil-pack sun-dried tomatoes, minced
8 fresh basil leaves, chopped
2 garlic cloves, minced
$1/4$ cup chopped pine nuts

For the crostini, arrange the baguette slices in a single layer on a baking parchment-lined baking sheet. Combine the olive oil, dill weed, thyme, rosemary and garlic in a small bowl and mix well. Brush over the tops of the baguette slices. Bake at 300 degrees for 30 minutes or until crisp but not brown.

For the tomato goat cheese spread, mash the goat cheese with a fork in a medium bowl. Add the tomatoes, basil, garlic and pine nuts and mix well. Chill, covered, for up to 4 days. Let stand at room temperature before serving. Spread on the crostini.

Makes 12 servings

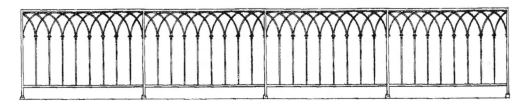

Fresh Figs with Rosemary Goat Cheese

11 ounces mild goat cheese, softened
1/2 cup heavy cream or whipping cream
2 teaspoons finely chopped fresh rosemary leaves, or to taste
1 tablespoon honey
Salt and pepper to taste
1 pound fresh figs, stemmed and cut in half lengthwise.

Whisk the goat cheese, cream, rosemary and honey together in a bowl until smooth. Season with salt and pepper. Spread on the cut side of each fig half. Serve at room temperature.

Makes 10 servings

Note: Make the rosemary goat cheese 1 day ahead and store it, covered, in the refrigerator. Bring to room temperature before spreading on the figs. For a variation, add chopped toasted walnuts to the goat cheese mixture.

"When men reach their sixties and retire, they go to pieces.
Women go right on cooking."
—*Gail Sheehy*

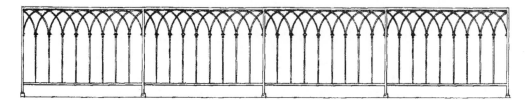

Tequila Margarita Cheese Ball

1 pound extra-sharp Cheddar cheese
4 to 6 garlic cloves, minced
1 bunch green onions, chopped (include the green tops)
2 tablespoons butter, softened
8 ounces cream cheese, softened
Grated zest of 2 oranges
1 1/2 teaspoons curry powder
1 1/2 teaspoons dry mustard
1 teaspoon coriander
1/2 teaspoon (or more) cayenne pepper
2 tablespoons gold tequila
2 tablespoons Cointreau
2 or 3 dried ancho chiles, stemmed, seeded and ground lightly in a spice
   grinder, or crushed red pepper or pure chile powder

Grate the cheese in a food processor. Add the garlic and green onions and pulse several times. Add the butter, cream cheese, orange zest, curry powder, dry mustard, coriander and cayenne pepper and pulse until mixed. Add the tequila and Cointreau slowly, processing constantly until smooth. Form the mixture into a ball. Chill, tightly covered in plastic wrap, until slightly firm. Form into the desired shape. Place the ancho chiles in a shallow bowl and coat the cheese mixture with them. Chill for 8 to 10 hours to allow the chiles to soften. Place on a serving plate and garnish with fresh cilantro and clusters of small dried red peppers. Serve with crisp garlic-flavored croutons or crackers.

Makes 15 to 20 servings

Note: This cheese ball gets better with age and keeps well in the refrigerator for several weeks. The recipe is from *The Herb Garden Cookbook* by Lucinda Hutson.

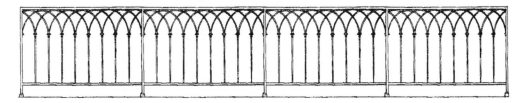

Hot Artichoke Dip

The classic version:
1 or 2 (14-ounce) cans artichoke hearts, drained
1 cup mayonnaise
1 cup (4 ounces) grated Parmesan cheese
1 teaspoon garlic powder (optional)
Dash of Worcestershire sauce (optional)
2 to 3 teaspoons chopped fresh dill weed, or
    1 teaspoon dried dill weed (optional)

The low-fat version:
1 (14-ounce) can artichoke hearts, drained
2 tablespoons Parmesan cheese
2 tablespoons low-fat sour cream or sour half-and-half
1 small garlic clove
1 teaspoon lemon juice
4 drops of hot red pepper sauce
3/4 cup plain yogurt
Paprika to taste

For the classic version, combine the artichoke hearts, mayonnaise and cheese in a food processor and process until the artichoke hearts are finely chopped. Combine the artichoke mixture, garlic powder, Worcestershire sauce and dill weed in a bowl and mix well. Pour into a buttered baking dish. Bake at 350 degrees for 20 minutes or until bubbly. Serve with melba rounds or chips.

Makes 20 to 25 servings

For the low-fat version, combine the artichoke hearts, cheese, sour cream, garlic, lemon juice and hot sauce in a food processor and process until the artichoke hearts are finely chopped. Combine the artichoke mixture and yogurt in a bowl and mix well. Pour into a buttered baking dish. Sprinkle with paprika. Bake at 350 degrees for 25 minutes or until bubbly. Serve with melba rounds or chips.

Makes 16 to 20 servings (2 cups)

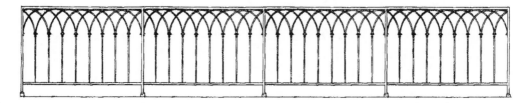

Crab and Brie Artichoke Dip

1 leek, trimmed, finely chopped,
   washed and drained
1 Vidalia or other sweet onion, finely chopped
2 tablespoons minced garlic
2 tablespoons olive oil
1/2 cup drained, canned artichoke hearts, finely chopped
1/2 cup frozen chopped spinach, thawed and squeezed dry
1/4 cup Riesling or other medium-dry white wine
2/3 cup heavy cream or whipping cream
1 pound Brie cheese, rind trimmed and
   cut into 1/4-inch pieces
3 tablespoons finely chopped fresh parsley
2 tablespoons finely chopped fresh dill weed
1 tablespoon finely chopped fresh tarragon
1 pound jumbo lump crab meat,
   shells removed and meat flaked
2 tablespoons Dijon mustard
1 teaspoon Tabasco sauce, or to taste
Salt and pepper to taste

Sauté the leek, onion and garlic in the olive oil in a heavy skillet, stirring until pale golden brown. Stir in the artichoke hearts and spinach. Add the wine. Cook for 3 minutes, stirring constantly. Add the cream and simmer for 1 minute longer. Add the Brie and stir until just beginning to melt. Remove the skillet from the heat and stir in the parsley, dill weed and tarragon. Combine the crab meat, Dijon mustard, Tabasco sauce, salt and pepper in a large bowl and mix well. Stir in the cheese mixture. Spread in a lightly oiled 11-inch gratin dish or other shallow 6-cup baking dish. Bake at 425 degrees for 15 to 20 minutes or until golden brown. Serve hot with toasted baguette slices.

Makes 6 to 8 servings

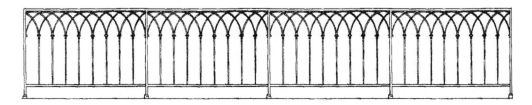

Hot Broccoli Dip

1/2 cup chopped onion
1/2 cup chopped celery
1/2 cup chopped fresh mushrooms
3 tablespoons butter
1 (10-ounce) package frozen broccoli, cooked, drained and chopped
1 (10-ounce) can cream of mushroom soup

1 (6-ounce) package garlic cheese, diced
Generous squeeze of lemon juice
3/4 cup almonds, sliced
1/4 cup water
1 teaspoon Worcestershire sauce
1/8 teaspoon Tabasco sauce
1/8 teaspoon pepper

Sauté the onion, celery and mushrooms in the butter in a skillet until tender. Add the broccoli, soup and cheese. Cook over low heat until the cheese is melted, stirring constantly. Add the lemon juice. Stir in the almonds, water, Worcestershire sauce, Tabasco sauce and pepper. Remove to a chafing dish. Serve with corn chips.

Makes 12 servings (3 to 4 cups)

Note: This recipe is from a Medical Auxiliary cookbook published many years ago. The dip continues to be a favorite at neighborhood brunches each holiday season.

Mexican Corn Dip

8 ounces cream cheese, softened
1/2 cup (1 stick) butter, softened
2 (11-ounce) cans Mexicorn or Shoe Peg corn
1 tablespoon chopped jalapeño chiles

Combine the cream cheese, butter, corn and chiles in a bowl and mix well. Spoon into a buttered baking dish. Bake at 350 degrees for 30 minutes. Serve hot with tortilla chips.

Makes 6 to 8 servings (2 cups)

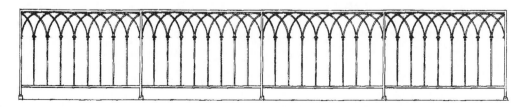

Texas Caviar

3 (15-ounce) cans black-eyed peas, drained
1 onion, chopped
Chopped red, yellow and green bell peppers to taste
1 (4-ounce) can diced green chiles
1 bottle zesty Italian salad dressing
Dash of hot red pepper sauce
1 bunch cilantro, chopped

Combine the black-eyed peas, onion, bell peppers, chiles, salad dressing, hot sauce and cilantro in a bowl and mix well. Marinate in the refrigerator for at least 3 hours. Serve with scoop-style corn chips.

Makes 8 servings

Black Bean Salsa

2 (15-ounce) cans black beans, drained and rinsed
1 (17-ounce) can whole kernel corn, drained
2 large tomatoes, chopped
1 large avocado, chopped
1 small red onion, chopped
1/4 cup chopped cilantro
1/4 cup lime juice
2 tablespoons olive oil
1 tablespoon red wine vinegar
1 teaspoon salt
1/2 teaspoon pepper

Combine the beans, corn, tomatoes, avocado, onion, cilantro, lime juice, olive oil, vinegar, salt and pepper in a large bowl and mix well. Chill, covered, until serving time. Serve with corn chips.

Makes 10 servings

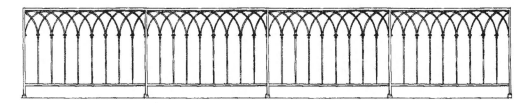

Hummus

2 garlic cloves
2 (15-ounce) cans chick-peas
1/3 cup tahini
Juice of 1 lemon
1/2 teaspoon salt
1/2 teaspoon paprika
1/2 teaspoon cumin
2 tablespoons olive oil

Chop the garlic in a food processor. Drain the chick-peas, reserving 1/3 cup of the liquid. Add the chick-peas to the food processor and process until smooth. Add the tahini and pulse several times. Add the lemon juice, reserved chick-pea liquid, salt, paprika and cumin and pulse several times. Add the olive oil and process until smooth. Store, covered, in the refrigerator for up to 1 week.

Makes 15 to 20 servings

Olive Tapenade

2 cans black olives (any size) packed in olive oil
2 ribs celery, coarsely chopped
1 carrot, coarsely chopped
5 to 10 garlic cloves, coarsely chopped
1/2 cup coarsely chopped fresh basil
1/4 cup coarsely chopped fresh oregano

Drain the olives, reserving the olive oil. Pit the olives if necessary. Combine the olives, celery, carrot, garlic, basil and oregano in a food processor. Pour the reserved olive oil over the top and process to a paste texture, scraping the side of the bowl several times. Remove to a serving dish. Serve with crusty bread, toast or hearty crackers.

Makes 10 servings

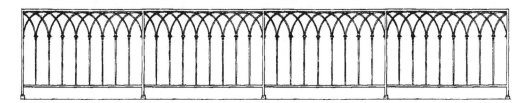

Old-Fashioned Eggnog

6 egg whites
2 cups heavy cream or whipping cream
6 egg yolks
1 cup sugar
2 cups bourbon
Freshly grated nutmeg

Beat the egg whites in a mixing bowl until stiff peaks form. Beat the cream in a mixing bowl until soft peaks form. Beat the egg yolks in a large bowl until thick and pale yellow. Add the sugar and beat until well incorporated. Beat in the bourbon. Fold in the egg whites. Fold in the whipped cream. Chill thoroughly before serving. Top each serving with grated nutmeg.

Makes 20 to 25 servings

Note: The contributor's grandmother, at age 18, worked as a pharmacy assistant at Searcy Hospital, where she was instructed by one of the doctors to make this eggnog recipe daily as a therapeutic treat for all the patients and himself.

Mock Champagne

2 quarts ginger ale, chilled
1 quart apple juice, chilled

Pour the ginger ale and apple juice over an ice ring containing lemons, limes and fresh mint leaves or serve from a silver or crystal pitcher.

Makes 20 to 25 servings

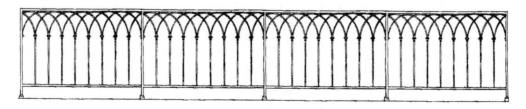

Garden Sangria

4 oranges, sliced
1 gallon dry red wine or fruity white wine
1 cup Grand Marnier or Cointreau
2 cups brandy
2 bunches long-stemmed lemon verbena and/or any
   combination of fresh mint, lemon balm and pineapple sage
Fresh seasonal fruits such as seedless grapes, apple, pear or
   peach slices, strawberries, star fruit and kiwifuit
2 lemons, thinly sliced
2 limes, thinly sliced
Additional sprigs of fresh herbs
2 (16-ounce) packages frozen peaches or frozen blueberries
Club soda, sparkling Spanish wine or Champagne

Combine the oranges, wine, Grand Marnier, brandy and fresh herbs in a large glass container. Chill, covered, for several days. Add any firm fruits, such as grapes and apples, and the lemons and limes 4 to 6 hours before serving. Pour the sangria into a glass pitcher, replacing the herb sprigs with fresh ones. Add any soft fruits such as strawberries. Add the frozen fruits just before serving to help keep the sangria chilled. Pour into long-stemmed glasses. Add a splash of club soda and a fresh herb sprig.

Makes 15 to 20 servings

Note: This recipe is from *The Herb Garden Cookbook* by Lucinda Hutson

Bridal Punch

1 gallon pineapple sherbet
3 quarts ginger ale, chilled
1 quart apple juice, chilled

Spoon the sherbet into a punch bowl. Pour the ginger ale and apple juice over the sherbet and stir gently.

Makes 40 servings

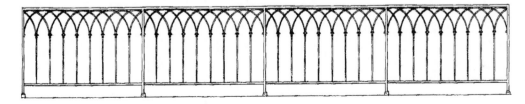

Spiked Cranberry Punch

2 cups cranberry juice
1 cup vodka
1/4 cup lime juice
1 cup ginger ale
4 teaspoons sugar

Combine the cranberry juice, vodka, lime juice, ginger ale and sugar in a pitcher and stir well. Pour over an ice ring in a punch bowl.

Makes 10 to 12 servings

Hot Holiday Punch

1/3 cup packed brown sugar
1 1/2 teaspoons whole cloves
1 1/2 teaspoons whole allspice
3 cinnamon sticks, broken into pieces
2 cups cranberry juice
2 cups pineapple juice
2 cups apple juice
1 cup water

Combine the brown sugar, cloves, allspice and cinnamon sticks in the basket of a coffee brewer. Add the cranberry juice, pineapple juice, apple juice and water to the water compartment of the brewer. Brew as for coffee.

Makes 8 to 10 servings

Note: Brewing this beverage makes the entire house smell festive. Increase the quantities and brew in a larger urn to serve more guests.

Wassail

2 quarts apple juice
2¹/4 cups pineapple juice
2 cups orange juice
1 cup lemon juice
¹/2 cup sugar
1 (3-inch) cinnamon stick
1 teaspoon whole cloves

Combine the apple juice, pineapple juice, orange juice, lemon juice, sugar, cinnamon stick and cloves in a Dutch oven. Bring to a boil. Reduce the heat and simmer, covered, for 20 minutes. Simmer, uncovered, for 20 minutes longer. Strain, discarding the cinnamon stick and cloves. Serve hot.

Makes 12 to 15 servings

Note: This drink will warm up your guests at any winter gathering. The spicy aroma will make the house smell wonderful.

Cocoa Mix

8 cups instant powdered milk
3/4 cup nondairy coffee creamer
2 cups instant cocoa mix

Combine the powdered milk, coffee creamer and cocoa mix in a large bowl and mix well. Store in an airtight container. Stir ¹/3 cup of the cocoa mix into 1 cup of boiling water for each serving. Top with marshmallows if desired.

Makes 30 servings

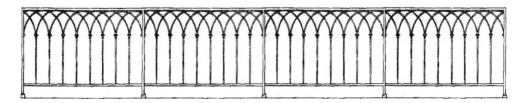

Brunch & Breads

"[Bread making is] one of those almost hypnotic businesses, like a dance from some ancient ceremony. It leaves you filled with one of the world's sweetest smells...."

M.F.K. Fisher, *The Art of Eating*

Shrimp and Grits Casserole

4 cups chicken broth
1 cup grits (not instant)
1 cup (4 ounces) shredded sharp Cheddar cheese
1 cup (4 ounces) shredded Monterey Jack cheese
6 green onions, chopped
1 green bell pepper, chopped
1 garlic clove, minced
2 tablespoons butter
1 pound fresh small shrimp, cooked and peeled
1 (10-ounce) can diced tomatoes with green chiles, drained
1/4 teaspoon pepper
1/4 cup shredded cheese

Bring the broth to a boil in a large saucepan. Stir in the grits. Reduce the heat and simmer, covered, for 20 minutes. Remove from the heat. Stir in 1 cup Cheddar cheese and 1 cup Monterey Jack cheese. Sauté the onions, bell pepper and garlic in the butter in a large skillet for 5 minutes or until tender. Stir into the grits mixture. Add the shrimp, tomatoes with green chiles and pepper and mix well. Pour into a lightly greased 2-quart baking dish. Top with 1/4 cup cheese. Bake, uncovered, at 350 degrees for 30 to 45 minutes.

Makes 10 to 12 servings

"Never trust a skinny cook."
—*Unknown*

Breakfast Casserole

1 pound bulk pork sausage
3 or 4 slices bread, cut into cubes
8 slices bacon, crisp-cooked and crumbled
6 eggs
2 cups milk
1 cup (4 ounces) shredded cheese
1 teaspoon salt
1 teaspoon dry mustard

Brown the sausage in a skillet, stirring until crumbly; drain. Arrange the bread cubes in a 10×13-inch baking dish. Top with the sausage and bacon. Combine the eggs, milk, cheese, salt and dry mustard in a bowl and mix well. Pour over the sausage and bacon. Bake at 350 degrees for 45 minutes.

Makes 10 to 12 servings

Note: Add a layer of chopped green or red bell peppers or onions to the casserole if you like. Prepare and chill the casserole the night before baking for a quick and easy brunch dish.

"Cooking is at once child's play and adult joy. And cooking
done with care is an act of love."
—*Craig Claiborne,* Kitchen Primer

Sausage Pinwheels

1 (2-sheet) package frozen puff pastry
1 pound mild or hot bulk pork sausage
Red pepper flakes (optional)
Chopped green onions (optional)
Shredded cheese (optional)

Let the puff pastry thaw for 30 minutes; unroll both sheets. Spread each sheet with 1/2 of the sausage. Sprinkle with red pepper flakes, green onions and shredded cheese. Roll from the long side to form 2 long thin logs. Wrap the logs tightly in plastic wrap; wrap again in foil. Store in the refrigerator or freezer until ready to bake. Cut both rolls into 1/2-inch slices. Bake at 400 degrees for 15 to 20 minutes.

Makes 25 to 30 servings

"No one who cooks, cooks alone. Even at her most solitary, a cook
in the kitchen is surrounded by generations of cooks past, the advice and
menus of cooks present, the wisdom of cookbook writers."
—Laurie Colwin

Fruit Salad

1 can pitted dark sweet cherries
1 can sliced peaches or apricots
2 large cans pineapple chunks
3 to 4 tablespoons all-purpose flour
3/4 cup sugar
1/2 cup (1 stick) butter, melted
1/3 package Waverly wafers, crumbled
2 tablespoons sugar
1 1/2 cups (6 ounces) shredded sharp Cheddar cheese

Drain the cherries in a colander; rinse with cold water. Drain the peaches. Drain the pineapple chunks, reserving 1 1/2 cups pineapple juice. Whisk the flour and 3/4 cup sugar into the pineapple juice in a large bowl, beating until the sugar is dissolved. Stir in the cherries, peaches and pineapple chunks. Pour into a 3-quart baking dish coated with nonstick cooking spray. Combine the butter, wafer crumbs and 2 tablespoons sugar in a small bowl and mix well. Stir in the cheese. Sprinkle over the fruit. Bake at 350 degrees until bubbly and slightly brown on top.

Makes 8 to 10 servings

"Tis an ill cook that cannot lick his own fingers."
—*William Shakespeare*, Romeo and Juliet

Crème Brûlée French Toast

1/2 cup (1 stick) butter
1 cup packed brown sugar
2 tablespoons light corn syrup
1 loaf country-style bread
5 eggs
1 1/2 cups half-and-half
1 tablespoon orange juice
1 teaspoon vanilla extract
1/4 teaspoon salt

Melt the butter with the brown sugar and corn syrup in a small heavy saucepan over medium heat, stirring until smooth. Pour into a 9×13-inch baking dish. Cut 6 (1-inch) slices from the center of the bread. Trim the crusts. Arrange the slices (left whole or cut into strips or cubes) over the butter mixture. Whisk the eggs, half-and-half, orange juice, vanilla and salt together in a bowl. Pour evenly over the bread. Chill, covered, for at least 8 hours. Bring to room temperature before baking. Bake, uncovered, on the middle rack of the oven at 350 degrees for 35 to 40 minutes or until puffed and pale golden brown. Serve immediately.

Makes 10 to 12 servings

"The fact is that it takes more than ingredients and technique
to cook a good meal. A good cook puts something of himself into the
preparatioon—he cooks with enjoyment, anticipation,
spontaneity, and he is willing to experiment.
—*Pearl Bailey*, Pearl's Kitchen (1973)

Apple Pecan Topping

3 tablespoons butter
1/4 cup pecans, chopped
2 cups thinly sliced peeled apples
1 cup maple syrup
1 teaspoon ground cinnamon
Dash of salt

Melt the butter in a skillet and stir in the pecans. Cook until slightly brown. Remove the pecans from the butter with a slotted spoon. Add the apples, maple syrup, cinnamon and salt to the butter in the skillet. Cook, covered, over low heat for 10 minutes. Stir in the pecans. Serve over French toast, pancakes or waffles.

Makes about 3 cups

Scuppernong Jelly

5 cups scuppernong grapes
1 package Sure-Jell
1 pat of butter
5 cups sugar

Cover the grapes with water in a saucepan. Bring to a boil. Reduce the heat to low and simmer for 30 minutes. Let stand until cool. Strain through a colander into a saucepan, pressing the skins to remove all the juices. Discard the skins. Add the Sure-Jell and butter. Bring to a boil. Cook for 1 minute. Add the sugar and stir until dissolved. Pour into hot sterilized jelly jars; seal with 2-piece lids.

Makes 4 (1/2-pint) jars

Note: Many Southerners lucky enough to have scuppernongs growing in their yard still gather the grapes towards summer's end to make scuppernong jelly.

Cheese Garlic Biscuits

2 cups baking mix
2/3 cup milk
1/2 cup (2 ounces) shredded Cheddar cheese
1/4 cup (1/2 stick) butter, melted
1/4 teaspoon garlic powder

Combine the baking mix, milk and cheese in a bowl, stirring to make a soft dough. Beat vigorously with a wooden spoon for 30 seconds. Drop by spoonfuls onto an ungreased baking sheet. Bake at 450 degrees for 8 to 10 minutes or until golden brown. Combine the butter and garlic powder in a small bowl. Brush over the warm biscuits.

Makes 10 to 12 biscuits

Ham and Cheese Biscuits

1/2 cup (1 stick) butter
3 tablespoons mustard
3 teaspoons sesame seeds
1 teaspoon Worcestershire sauce
2 packages party rolls, split horizontally
2 packages brown sugar ham
1 large package shredded Swiss cheese
1 small onion, grated

Melt the butter with the mustard, sesame seeds and Worcestershire sauce in a small saucepan, stirring well. Spread over the bottom half of the rolls. Top with the ham, cheese and onion. Cover with the roll tops. Bake at 350 degrees for 20 minutes.

Makes 40 biscuits

Orange Puffs

1/4 cup (1/2 stick) margarine
1/2 cup sugar
1/3 cup orange juice
Grated orange zest (optional)
1 can refrigerator biscuits

Combine the margarine, sugar, orange juice and orange zest in a saucepan. Bring to a boil. Reduce the heat and simmer for 3 minutes. Pour a little of the orange sauce into each of 12 muffin cups, reserving a little sauce to drizzle over the baked puffs. Make a hole through the center of each biscuit and place over the sauce in the muffin cups. Bake the biscuits according to the package directions. Invert onto a serving plate. Drizzle with the remaining sauce.

Makes 12 servings

Note: These orange biscuits are as good as any you can buy. They are quick and easy and made from ingredients likely to be on hand. Try them when you need extra bread for unexpected company.

Blueberry Corn Muffins

1 cup cornmeal
1 cup all-purpose flour
1/2 cup sugar
2 1/2 teaspoons baking powder
1/4 teaspoon salt
1 cup buttermilk
6 tablespoons unsalted butter, melted
1 egg, lightly beaten
1 2/3 cups fresh blueberries or frozen blueberries, drained
1/2 teaspoon grated lemon zest

Sift the cornmeal, flour, sugar, baking powder and salt into a mixing bowl.
Make a well in the center of the dry ingredients and stir in the buttermilk,
butter and egg just until mixed. Fold in the blueberries and lemon zest.
Fill 12 greased or paper-lined muffin cups. Bake at 400 degrees for 20 to
25 minutes or until the muffins test done.

Makes 12 muffins

"A messy kitchen is a happy kitchen and this kitchen is delirious."
—*Unknown*

Orange Pecan Muffins

1/2 cup (1 stick) butter, softened
1 cup sugar
2 eggs
Grated zest of 1 orange
2 cups all-purpose flour
1 teaspoon baking soda
1/4 teaspoon salt
1 cup buttermilk
3/4 cup pecans, chopped
1/4 cup orange juice
1 tablespoon sugar

Cream the butter and 1 cup sugar in a mixing bowl until light and fluffy.
Beat in the eggs and orange zest. Stir in the flour, baking soda, salt and
buttermilk. Fold in the pecans. Fill 6 large or 12 regular-size greased or
paper-lined muffin cups. Bake at 375 degrees for 20 to 25 minutes or until
the muffins test done. Brush the orange juice over the warm muffins. Sprinkle
with 1 tablespoon sugar.

Makes 6 large or 12 regular-size muffins

Pecan Pie Muffins

1 cup pecans, chopped
1 cup packed dark brown sugar
1/2 cup all-purpose flour
2 eggs
1/2 cup (1 stick) margarine, melted

Combine the pecans, brown sugar and flour in a bowl and mix well. Beat the
eggs with the margarine in a small bowl. Add to the pecan mixture and stir
just until mixed. Spoon into greased muffin cups. Bake at 350 degrees for
20 minutes for regular-size muffins or 10 minutes for miniature muffins.

Makes 12 regular-size muffins or 20 miniature muffins

Chocolate Chip Banana Nut Bread

3 ripe bananas
1/2 cup (1 stick) butter, softened
2 cups all-purpose flour
1 cup sugar
1 teaspoon baking powder
1 teaspoon baking soda
1/2 teaspoon salt
1/4 teaspoon vanilla extract
2 eggs
1 cup (6 ounces) chocolate chips
1/2 cup chopped pecans (optional)

Grease and flour a 5×7-inch loaf pan; line the bottom with waxed paper.
Mash the bananas and butter together in a large mixing bowl. Add the flour,
sugar, baking powder, baking soda, salt and vanilla and mix well. Beat in the
eggs. Stir in the chocolate chips and pecans. Pour into the prepared pan.
Bake at 325 degrees for 55 minutes or until a crust begins to form on top.
Remove from the pan. Let cool on a wire rack.

Makes 1 loaf

Note: The addition of chocolate chips to a traditional banana nut bread
will satisfy the chocoholics in your family.

Pumpkin Bread

1¹/₃ cups all-purpose flour
1¹/₂ cups sugar
1 teaspoon baking soda
³/₄ teaspoon salt
1¹/₂ teaspoons ground cinnamon
Generous grating of fresh nutmeg, or
   ¹/₄ teaspoon ground nutmeg
¹/₂ teaspoon ground ginger
1 cup canned pumpkin
2 eggs
¹/₂ cup canola oil or other neutral vegetable oil
¹/₂ cup water

Combine the flour, sugar, baking soda, salt, cinnamon, nutmeg and ginger in a mixing bowl and stir well. Beat the pumpkin, eggs, canola oil and water together in a bowl. Add to the dry ingredients and stir just until mixed. Pour into a greased and floured 5x7-inch loaf pan. Bake at 350 degrees for 1 hour or until the top is firm. Let cool on a wire rack.

Makes 1 loaf

Note: Vary the recipe to suit your taste by adding chopped nuts, raisins or chocolate chips.

Bubble Bread

1 package frozen dinner roll dough
1 cup packed brown sugar
$1/2$ cup (1 stick) butter, melted
$1/2$ (4-ounce) package cook-and-serve
   butterscotch pudding mix
1 cup pecan halves
$1/4$ cup cinnamon-sugar
$1/2$ cup light corn syrup

Arrange the frozen rolls in a greased bundt pan. Sprinkle with the brown sugar.
Pour the butter evenly over the rolls. Sprinkle the pudding mix, pecans,
cinnamon-sugar and corn syrup over the rolls. Let rise, tightly covered with
foil, for 8 to 12 hours. Remove foil and bake at 350 degrees for 35 minutes or
until the rolls are brown. Invert onto a serving platter.

Makes 8 servings

"I cook with wine . . . sometimes I even put it in food."
—*Unknown*

Jalapeño Cheese Corn Bread

1 1/2 cups self-rising cornmeal
1/3 cup all-purpose flour
1/2 teaspoon garlic salt
2 eggs, beaten
1 can cream-style corn
1/4 cup chopped jalapeño chiles
1 cup buttermilk
3 tablespoons canola oil
2 cups (8 ounces) shredded sharp Cheddar cheese

Combine the cornmeal, flour and garlic salt in a large bowl and mix well. Beat the eggs, corn, jalapeño chiles, buttermilk and canola oil together in a bowl. Add to the dry ingredients and mix well. Layer the batter and cheese 1/2 at a time in a 7×12-inch baking dish. Bake at 350 degrees for 40 to 45 minutes or until set and light brown. Cool for 5 minutes. Cut into squares.

Makes 6 to 8 servings

"If you can't stand the heat, get out of the kitchen."
—*Harry S. Truman* (1884–1972)

Double Corn Spoon Bread with Chiles and Cheese

8 eggs, beaten
2 (16-ounce) cans cream-style corn
2 cups (8 ounces) shredded medium-sharp Cheddar cheese, or
   Monterey Jack cheese or a mixture of both
1¹/2 cups yellow cornmeal, preferably stone-ground
1 (4-ounce) can diced green chiles, drained
2 (4-ounce) jars diced roasted red peppers, drained and rinsed
²/3 cup buttermilk
¹/2 cup sugar
2 to 5 pickled jalapeño chiles, stemmed and minced
2 teaspoons baking powder
1¹/2 teaspoons baking soda
1¹/2 teaspoons salt

Whisk the eggs, corn and cheese together in a large mixing bowl. Stir in the cornmeal, green chiles, red peppers and buttermilk. Add the sugar, jalapeño chiles, baking powder, baking soda and salt and mix well. Pour into a buttered 9×13-inch baking dish. Bake at 375 degrees for 35 to 40 minutes or until puffed and barely set in the center. Serve hot or warm.

Makes 10 servings

Note: The bread is spoonable when it is hot but will firm up as it cools. This is great served with chili.

Italian Easter Bread

5 cups sifted all-purpose flour
1/2 cup sugar
2 tablespoons grated lemon zest
1 teaspoon salt
2 envelopes dry yeast
1/2 cup milk
1/2 cup water

1/2 cup (1 stick) butter or
  margarine, softened
2 eggs
1/2 cup golden raisins (optional)
12 eggs, uncooked and dyed with
  Easter egg dye coloring
2 egg whites, beaten

Combine 1 1/2 cups of the flour, the sugar, lemon zest, salt and yeast in a large mixing bowl. Heat the milk, water and butter to 125 degrees in a small saucepan over moderately low heat. Add gradually to the flour mixture. Beat at medium speed for 2 minutes, scraping the bowl occasionally. Add 2 eggs and 3/4 cup of the flour, or enough to make a thick batter. Beat at high speed for 2 minutes, scraping the bowl occasionally with a spoon. Add enough of the remaining flour to make a soft dough. Knead on a floured surface for 8 to 10 minutes or until smooth and elastic. Place in a greased bowl, turning to coat the surface. Let rise, covered with a damp towel, in a warm place for 1 to 1 1/2 hours or until doubled in bulk. Punch down the dough. Knead in the raisins on a floured surface. Let rise, covered, for 15 minutes.

Divide the dough into 4 equal portions. Roll each portion into a 28-inch rope. Loosely twist 2 of the ropes together 6 times on a greased baking sheet. Shape into a ring and seal the ends together. Insert a colored egg between each of the 6 twists of the ropes. Make a second ring with the remaining ropes and eggs. Cover the rings with a sheet of waxed paper and a tea towel. Let rise in a warm place for 30 to 40 minutes or until doubled in bulk. Brush the rings with the egg whites, being careful not to brush the eggs. Bake at 375 degrees for 25 to 30 minutes or until golden brown. Serve hot. Include an egg in each portion of bread.

Makes 12 servings

Note: This delightful bread recipe has been passed down through the generations. Children enjoy helping to dye the eggs to be used in the bread as well as helping to braid the bread into rings and other shapes.

Stout Beer Batter Bread

3 cups all-purpose flour
1/4 cup sugar
1 tablespoon baking powder
1 teaspoon salt
12 ounces beer
1/2 cup (1 stick) butter, melted

Combine the flour, sugar, baking powder and salt in a large bowl. Stir in the beer. Pour into a greased 5x7-inch loaf pan. Pour the butter over the top. Bake at 350 degrees for 45 minutes or until a knife inserted in the center comes out clean. Remove from the oven. Cool for 5 minutes. Invert the loaf onto a wire rack. Let stand upside down until cool.

Makes 1 loaf

Note: When making multiple batches, you may want to substitute some water for part of the beer so that the beer flavor does not become overwhelming. This bread makes a great grilled cheese sandwich. It's also good with pimento cheese.

"The kitchen is a country in which there are
always discoveries to be made."
—*Grimod de la Reyniere* (1758–1838)

Soups & Salads

"Of soup and love, the first is best."
old spanish proverb

Tomato Dill Bisque

2 onions, chopped
1 garlic clove, sliced
2 tablespoons margarine
4 large tomatoes (2 pounds), peeled and cubed
1/2 cup water
1 chicken bouillon cube
2 1/4 teaspoons fresh dill weed, or
  3/4 teaspoon dried dill weed
1/4 teaspoon salt
1/8 teaspoon pepper
1/2 cup mayonnaise

Sauté the onions and garlic in the margarine in a saucepan over medium heat for 3 minutes. Stir in the tomatoes, water, bouillon cube, dill weed, salt and pepper. Simmer, covered, for 10 minutes. Let stand until cool. Purée in 2 batches in a blender. Pour into a large container and stir in the mayonnaise. Chill, covered, for 8 or more hours.

Makes 4 to 6 servings

Note: This is a nice soup to make in the summer when good tomatoes are plentiful.

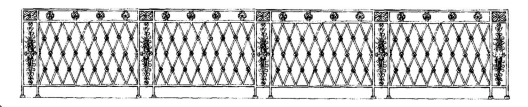

Gazpacho

2 cups tomato juice
1 cup chopped peeled tomatoes
1/2 cup chopped green bell pepper
1/2 cup chopped celery
1/2 cup chopped cucumber
1/2 cup chopped carrots
1/4 cup chopped onion
2 garlic cloves, minced
3 tablespoons wine vinegar
2 tablespoons olive oil
1 teaspoon salt
1/4 teaspoon pepper
1/2 teaspoon Worcestershire sauce

Combine the tomato juice, tomatoes, bell pepper, celery, cucumber, carrots, onion, garlic, vinegar, olive oil, salt, pepper and Worcestershire sauce in a large bowl and mix well. Purée 1/2 of the vegetable mixture in a blender. Pour back into the remaining vegetable mixture and stir well. Chill for at least 4 hours before serving.

Makes 6 servings

Note: This soup keeps in the refrigerator for days. It makes good use of summer's garden bounty.

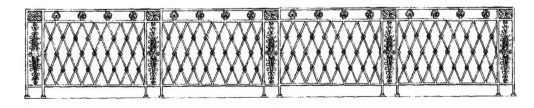

Seven Onion Soup with Parmesan Garlic Bread

1/4 cup (1/2 stick) unsalted butter
4 slices bacon, chopped
1 1/2 cups sliced yellow onions
1 1/2 cups sliced red onions
1 1/2 cups sliced white onions
1 cup sliced shallots
1 bay leaf
1/2 teaspoon thyme
1/2 teaspoon salt
1/2 teaspoon freshly ground pepper
1 cup sliced leeks (bottoms only), well rinsed

1 cup sliced scallions (white parts only)
1/3 cup all-purpose flour
2 quarts chicken stock
1 cup heavy cream or whipping cream
Salt and pepper to taste
3 teaspoons snipped chives
Shaved Parmesan cheese
Parmesan Garlic Bread (page 53)

Melt the butter in a soup pot over medium-high heat. Add the bacon. Cook for 7 minutes or until crisp. Remove the bacon with a slotted spoon. Add the yellow onions, red onions, white onions, shallots, bay leaf, thyme, 1/2 teaspoon salt and 1/2 teaspoon pepper to the bacon drippings. Cook for 8 to 10 minutes or until the onions are very soft and beginning to caramelize, stirring constantly. Add the leeks and scallions. Cook for 3 to 4 minutes or until tender. Sprinkle with the flour. Cook until the flour turns a light golden brown, stirring constantly. Add the stock and bring to a boil. Reduce the heat and simmer, uncovered, for 45 minutes, stirring occasionally. Stir in the cream and salt and pepper to taste. Cook over low heat for 15 minutes longer or until heated through. Remove and discard the bay leaf. Purée the soup with an immersion blender. Heat gently, stirring constantly. Garnish each serving with the bacon, chives and shaved Parmesan cheese. Serve with slices of Parmesan Garlic Bread.

Makes 8 servings

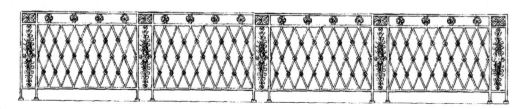

Parmesan Garlic Bread

1/2 cup (1 stick) unsalted butter, softened
1 tablespoon minced garlic
1 teaspoon chopped fresh chives
1 1/2 teaspoons chopped fresh parsley
1/4 teaspoon salt
1/8 teaspoon freshly ground pepper
1/2 cup (2 ounces) freshly grated Parmigiano-Reggiano
1 (12- to 14-inch) French baguette,
  ends trimmed and cut in half lengthwise

Cream the butter, garlic, chives, parsley, salt, pepper and 1/2 of the cheese in a small bowl, using a wooden spoon or rubber spatula. Spread over both halves of the baguette. Top with the remaining cheese. Place cut sides up on a foil-lined baking sheet. Bake at 350 degrees for 12 to 15 minutes or until fragrant and lightly golden brown around the edges. You may also broil for 1 to 2 minutes or until golden brown. Cut diagonally into 1/2-inch slices. Serve hot.

Makes 8 servings

"Soup is cuisine's kindest course. It breathes reassurance; it steams consolation; after a weary day it promotes sociability, as the five o'clock cup of tea or the cocktail hour."
—*Louis P. De Goury*, The Soup Book (1949)

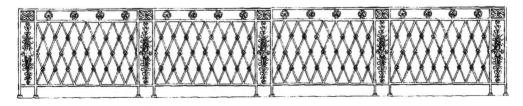

curried Pumpkin Soup

1 large onion, sliced
3/4 cup sliced scallions (white parts only)
1/4 cup (1/2 stick) unsalted butter
1 (16-ounce) can pumpkin (not pie filling)
4 cups chicken broth
1 bay leaf
1/2 teaspoon sugar
1/2 teaspoon curry powder
1/8 teaspoon nutmeg
Several parsley sprigs
2 cups half-and-half (not fat-free)
Salt and pepper to taste

Sauté the onion and scallions in the butter in a soup pot until light brown. Stir in the pumpkin, broth, bay leaf, sugar, curry powder, nutmeg and parsley sprigs. Bring to a boil. Reduce the heat and simmer, uncovered, for 15 minutes, stirring occasionally. Remove and discard the bay leaf. Let the soup stand until cool. Purée in batches in a blender. Pour back into the soup pot. Add the half-and-half, salt and pepper. Simmer for 5 to 10 minutes or until heated through. Garnish each serving with sour cream or heavy cream, chopped chives or a sprinkling of toasted pumpkin seeds.

Makes 6 servings

Note: This soup may be prepared a day in advance through the purée step, then chilled until serving time. Add the half-and-half to the cold soup and heat very slowly. Do not allow it to boil.

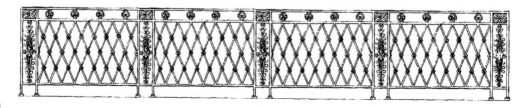

Red Pepper Soup

4 red bell peppers, chopped
1 onion, chopped
4 garlic cloves, minced
2 tablespoons butter

3 cups chicken broth
$^1/_2$ cup heavy cream or
   whipping cream
$^1/_8$ teaspoon pepper

Sauté the bell peppers, onion and garlic in the butter in a large saucepan for 5 to 10 minutes or until tender. Stir in the broth. Bring to a boil. Reduce the heat and simmer for 30 minutes. Purée in batches in a blender. Strain the soup into a saucepan and discard the solids. Add the cream and pepper to the soup. Cook over medium-low heat for 5 minutes or until heated through, stirring constantly.

Makes 5 servings

Note: Using roasted peppers rather than raw will improve the texture and flavor of the soup. Roast the whole peppers on the grill, remove the skins and chop.

Acorn Squash and Leek Soup

1 acorn squash (or pumpkin),
   peeled and cubed
2 leeks (white parts only), chopped
2 potatoes, peeled and cubed
1$^1/_2$ cups chicken broth or
   vegetable stock

$^1/_2$ cup any basic soup stock or broth
1 teaspoon bouquet garni (mixture
   of dried basil, parsley, rosemary,
   sage and thyme)
2 tablespoons butter or margarine
Juice of $^1/_2$ large lemon

Combine the squash, leeks, potatoes, broth, soup stock and bouquet garni in a large saucepan. Bring to a boil. Reduce the heat and simmer for 20 minutes or until the vegetables are tender. Remove and discard the bouquet garni. Remove the vegetables from the broth. Combine the vegetables, butter and lemon juice in a food processor and blend until smooth. Return the broth to a simmer and stir in the vegetable purée. Serve immediately or keep warm in a double boiler. Garnish each serving with chopped fresh herbs.

Makes 4 servings

Note: Serve with warm bread, salad and a crisp white wine.

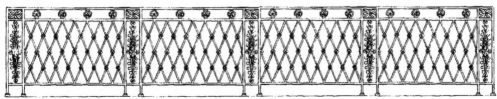

Baked Butternut Squash Soup

2 butternut squash (about 3 pounds),
  halved lengthwise and seeded
2 tablespoons butter, melted
Salt and pepper to taste
2 onions, chopped
1 Granny Smith apple, peeled, cored and chopped
2 garlic cloves, minced
Vegetable oil
3 tablespoons all-purpose flour
$1/4$ teaspoon freshly grated nutmeg
5 cups chicken broth
1 cup milk
Grated zest and juice of 1 orange
$1/2$ teaspoon salt
$1/2$ teaspoon pepper
Chopped fresh parsley

Brush the cut sides of the squash with the butter and season with salt and
pepper to taste. Bake cut side down on a foil-lined baking sheet at
450 degrees for 30 minutes. Turn squash over. Bake for 30 minutes longer or
until tender. Let stand until cool. Scoop the squash from the shell and chop;
discard the shell. Sauté the onions, apple and garlic in a little oil in a soup
pot over medium heat until tender. Stir in the flour and nutmeg. Add
the broth and milk slowly. Stir in the orange zest and juice, $1/2$ teaspoon salt
and $1/2$ teaspoon pepper. Bring to a boil. Reduce the heat and simmer,
covered, for 20 to 30 minutes. Let stand until cool. Purée in batches in a
blender or food processor. Garnish each serving with parsley.

Makes 8 to 10 servings

Note: This soup has a nice flavor and is easy to make. Add more butternut
squash and less grated orange zest if you like.

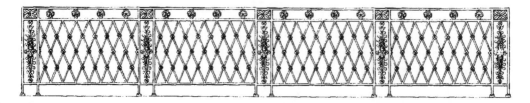

Green Tomato Soup

12 green tomatoes, quartered
1/2 cup chopped onion
1/2 cup thinly sliced leek
1/2 cup sliced celery
4 garlic cloves, crushed
1/2 cup olive oil
1 teaspoon sugar
Dash of hot red pepper sauce
Salt and pepper to taste
1 quart chicken stock
1 teaspoon fresh thyme leaves
1 teaspoon cumin
1/2 cup crème fraîche or sour cream
Sprigs of fresh flat-leaf parsley

Combine the tomatoes, onion, leek, celery, garlic, olive oil, sugar, hot sauce, salt and pepper in a large baking pan and toss well. Bake, covered with foil, at 350 degrees for 40 minutes or until the tomatoes are soft. Drain off any excess oil. Let stand until cool. Purée the vegetables with the stock in batches in a blender. Strain through a sieve into a soup pot and discard the solids. Add the thyme and cumin. Bring to a boil. Reduce the heat and simmer for 5 minutes. Adjust the salt and pepper to taste. Top each serving with a spoonful of crème fraîche and a sprig of parsley. Serve warm.

Makes 8 servings

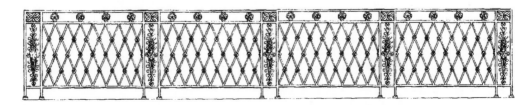

Creamy Chicken Soup

4 small cans boned chicken
2 (10-ounce) cans cream of mushroom soup
1 (14-ounce) can chicken broth
2 cups (or more) instant rice
2 cups water
2 cups half-and-half
1 tablespoon curry powder

Combine the chicken, soup, broth, rice, water, half-and-half and curry powder in a soup pot. Bring to a simmer, stirring constantly. Cover and let stand for 30 minutes.

Makes 8 to 10 servings

Note: This soup is easy to make and great served with biscuits on a cold winter day or night. It has been served as part of a neighborhood brunch for years. Mugs of the soup were followed by ham and cheese biscuits, hot broccoli dip with corn chips, fresh strawberries with whipped cream, lemon squares, and hot percolator punch.

"In the childhood memories of every *good cook*, there's a large kitchen, a warm stove, a simmering pot and a mom."
—*Barbara Costikyan*

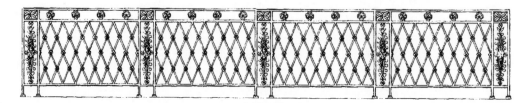

Santa Fe Soup

2 pounds ground turkey or
   ground beef
1 large onion, chopped
2 envelopes ranch salad dressing mix
2 envelopes taco seasoning mix
2 (16-ounce) cans white corn
1 (16-ounce) can black beans

1 (16-ounce) can kidney beans
1 (16-ounce) can pinto beans
1 (16-ounce) can diced tomatoes
1 (16-ounce) can diced tomatoes
   with green chiles
2 cups water

Brown the ground turkey with the onion in a soup pot, stirring until the ground turkey is crumbly; drain. Stir in the ranch salad dressing mix and taco seasoning mix. Add the corn, black beans, kidney beans, pinto beans, tomatoes, tomatoes with green chiles (including the juices from all the cans) and water. Bring to a boil. Reduce the heat and simmer for 2 hours, adding more water if soup becomes too thick. Garnish each serving with sour cream, shredded Cheddar cheese and chopped green onions. Serve with tortilla chips.

Makes 12 to 16 servings

Note: Even picky children will like this soup. It's a good dish for potluck suppers or to take to a friend.

Maine Fish Chowder

2 small cans chicken broth
2 to 4 potatoes, cubed
2 ribs celery, finely chopped
1 small onion, finely chopped
2 garlic cloves, crushed
1 teaspoon thyme

1/2 teaspoon pepper
1 cup corn kernels
1 pound whitefish, cut into
   small chunks
1 tablespoon butter
1 1/2 to 2 cups half-and-half or milk

Combine the broth, potatoes, celery, onion, garlic, thyme and pepper in a soup pot. Bring to a boil. Reduce the heat and simmer until the vegetables are tender. Stir in the corn and return to a simmer. Add the fish and butter. Simmer for 5 minutes or until the fish is cooked through. Stir in the half-and-half. Cook until heated through. Serve immediately.

Makes 6 to 10 servings

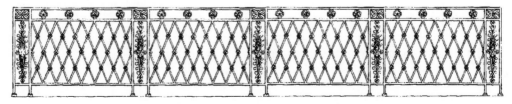

Poblano corn chowder with shrimp

2 tablespoons butter, softened
2 tablespoons all-purpose flour
1 onion, chopped
3 ribs celery, chopped
2 large poblano chiles, seeded and chopped
2 tablespoons butter
2 (15-ounce) cans cream-style corn
1 (16-ounce) package frozen corn kernels, thawed
2 (14-ounce) cans chicken broth
1 cup heavy cream or whipping cream
2 teaspoons sugar
1/2 teaspoon cayenne pepper
1 pound uncooked shrimp, peeled and deveined
6 tablespoons chopped cilantro
Salt and black pepper to taste

Combine 2 tablespoons butter and the flour in a small bowl and mix well. Sauté the onion, celery and chiles in 2 tablespoons butter in a soup pot for 6 minutes or until the vegetables are tender. Add the cream-style corn, corn kernels, broth, cream, sugar and cayenne pepper. Bring to a boil. Whisk in the butter and flour mixture. Simmer for 15 minutes. Add the shrimp and 4 tablespoons of the cilantro. Simmer for 5 minutes or until the shrimp are cooked. Season with salt and black pepper. Garnish each serving with the remaining cilantro.

Makes 6 to 12 servings

Note: This recipe is from the Sundown Café in Atlanta, Georgia.

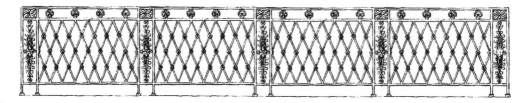

chicken and Sausage Gumbo

1 package chicken breasts with bones
1 package chicken thighs with bones
Salt, black pepper and cayenne pepper to taste
1 pound andouille (or other) sausage, casings removed and
   sausage chopped
2 cups okra
1 bell pepper, chopped
1 large onion, chopped
3 garlic cloves, minced
3 bay leaves
1 tablespoon poultry seasoning
Hot cooked rice

Combine the chicken breasts, chicken thighs, salt, black pepper, cayenne pepper and water to cover in a soup pot. Cook until the chicken is tender. Remove the chicken from the stock and let cool; reserve the stock. Sliver the chicken, discarding the bones. Brown the sausage in a large skillet. Remove the sausage, leaving the drippings in the skillet. Sauté the okra, bell pepper, onion, garlic, bay leaves and poultry seasoning in the drippings for 15 minutes or until the vegetables are tender, stirring frequently. Remove and discard the bay leaf. Add the vegetables to the chicken stock. Stir in the sausage and chicken. Simmer for 2 to 3 hours. Serve over hot cooked rice.

Makes 12 servings

Note: Gumbo is a personal thing. Vary the amount of ingredients according to taste. The amount of stock depends on the amount of water you use to cook the chicken.

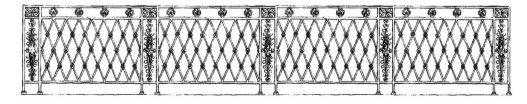

Tarragon Chicken Salad

1 large onion, thinly sliced
$1/2$ cup chopped fresh herbs
1 pound boneless skinless chicken breasts
Juice of 1 lemon
Kosher salt and pepper to taste
$2/3$ cup chopped celery
$1/2$ cup dried cranberries
$1/2$ cup chopped toasted pecans or pine nuts
$1/2$ cup sour cream (may use low-fat)
1 small shallot, finely chopped
1 tablespoon finely chopped fresh tarragon leaves

Layer the onion slices, $1/2$ cup herbs and the chicken breasts in a shallow roasting pan coated with nonstick cooking spray. Squeeze the lemon juice over the chicken and season with salt and pepper. Bake at 375 degrees for 35 minutes. Let cool. Chop the chicken and discard the onion. Combine the chicken, celery, cranberries, pecans, sour cream, shallot, tarragon leaves, salt and pepper in a bowl and mix well. Chill for several hours or overnight. Serve with a sturdy country bread or brown bread.

Makes 4 to 6 servings

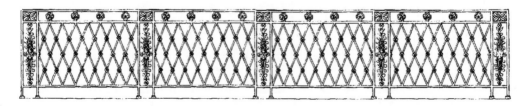

Wild Rice Chicken Salad

1 (6-ounce) package long grain
   wild rice, cooked
3 or 4 chicken breasts, cooked and
   diced
1 bunch green onions, chopped
1 red bell pepper, diced
1/3 cup seasoned white rice
   wine vinegar
1/3 cup canola oil or other
   vegetable oil

2 garlic cloves, minced
1 tablespoon Dijon mustard
1/2 teaspoon sugar
1/2 teaspoon salt
1/4 teaspoon pepper
2 avocados, cut into chunks and
   sprinkled with the juice of 1 lemon
1 cup chopped toasted pecans

Combine the wild rice, chicken, onions and bell pepper in a salad bowl.
Combine the vinegar, canola oil, garlic, Dijon mustard, sugar, salt and pepper
in a jar and shake well. Pour over the salad and toss to combine. Chill,
covered, for at least 3 hours. Add the avocados and pecans just before
serving and toss gently.

Makes 6 servings

Shrimp Lorenzo

3 avocados, peeled, halved and pits
   removed, or a large cucumber,
   cut in half lengthwise and seeded
18 cooked large shrimp
1 cup vegetable oil
6 tablespoons wine vinegar
1/3 cup chili sauce

1/4 cup chopped watercress
2 teaspoons chopped scallions
1 teaspoon tarragon
1 teaspoon dry mustard
1 teaspoon salt
1 teaspoon pepper

Arrange the avocado halves on 6 salad plates. Arrange 3 shrimp in each
avocado half. Combine the oil, vinegar, chili sauce, watercress, scallions,
tarragon, dry mustard, salt and pepper in a jar and shake well. Pour over the
avocados and shrimp. Garnish each salad with lemon wedges, watercress
and freshly ground pepper.

Makes 6 servings

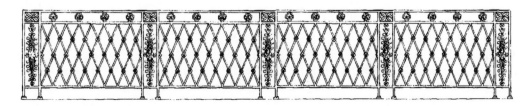

Greek Shrimp Salad

4 cups mixed baby lettuce
1 romaine heart, torn into
  bite-size pieces
1/2 cup cubed red bell pepper
1/2 cup cubed yellow bell pepper
1/2 cup Caramelized Onions (page 65)
1/2 cup kalamata olives, pitted
1 small cucumber, peeled,
  seeded, quartered, and cut
  into 1/2-inch slices
1 cup mixed golden pear tomatoes
  and Sweet 100 cherry tomatoes,
  cut into halves

1/2 cup (2 ounces) freshly grated
  Parmesan cheese
1 cup (4 ounces) crumbled feta
  cheese
1 cup Greek Salad Dressing (page 65)
Kosher salt to taste
Freshly ground pepper to taste
16 large shrimp, peeled, deveined,
  cut in half lengthwise and
  blanched
Shrimp Dressing (below)
1/4 cup pine nuts
Sprigs of dill weed

Combine the lettuce, bell peppers, Caramelized Onions, olives, cucumber, tomatoes, cheese and Greek Salad Dressing in a salad bowl and toss to combine. Season with salt and pepper. Divide among 4 chilled salad plates. Mix the shrimp and Shrimp Dressing in a bowl. Arrange 8 shrimp halves over each salad mound. Toast the pine nuts in a single layer in a skillet over low heat for 4 minutes or until golden brown, stirring often. Sprinkle over the salads. Garnish with dill weed.

Makes 4 servings

Shrimp Dressing

1/2 cup plain yogurt
2 tablespoons fresh lemon juice
2 tablespoons diced, seeded,
  peeled cucumber
1 tablespoon minced red onion

1 tablespoon minced fresh dill weed
1 teaspoon minced garlic
Kosher salt to taste
Pinch of cayenne pepper
Freshly ground black pepper to taste

Whisk the yogurt, lemon juice, cucumber, red onion, dill weed and garlic together in a bowl. Season with salt, cayenne pepper and black pepper. Chill, covered, until ready to use. Whisk again before serving.

Makes about 3/4 cup

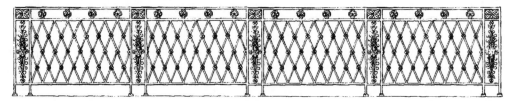

Greek Salad Dressing

1 cup plain yogurt
1/3 cup fresh lemon juice
1/4 cup red wine vinegar
1/4 cup Dijon mustard
2 tablespoons minced garlic
1 tablespoon minced fresh dill weed
1 tablespoon minced fresh parsley
1 tablespoon minced fresh thyme
1/2 teaspoon kosher salt
1/4 teaspoon freshly ground
    white pepper
1 1/2 cups extra-virgin olive oil
Sugar to taste

Whisk the yogurt, lemon juice, vinegar, Dijon mustard, garlic, dill weed, parsley, thyme, salt and white pepper together in a bowl. Add the olive oil a little at a time, whisking constantly until emulsified. Beat in a little sugar. Chill, covered, until ready to use. Whisk again before serving.

Makes about 3 cups

Caramelized Onions

1 large (3/4-pound) red, yellow or
    white onion, diced
2 tablespoons extra-virgin olive oil
2 tablespoons balsamic vinegar
Kosher salt to taste
Freshly ground pepper to taste

Sauté the onion in the olive oil in a skillet over medium heat for 15 minutes or until light brown, stirring frequently. Stir in the vinegar. Cook for 1 minute longer. Season with salt and pepper. Let cool. Store, covered, in the refrigerator. Use as needed.

Makes about 1 cup

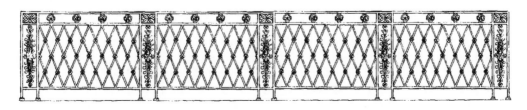

Caesar Salad with Sourdough Croutons

2 large heads romaine, torn into bite-size pieces
1 red onion, thinly sliced
Sourdough Croutons (below)
1/2 cup fresh lemon juice
2 tablespoons Worcestershire sauce
4 garlic cloves, coarsely chopped
1/2 teaspoon hot red pepper sauce
Salt and pepper to taste
1 cup olive oil
1 cup (4 ounces) freshly grated Parmesan cheese

Combine the lettuce, onion and Sourdough Croutons in a large salad bowl. Combine the lemon juice, Worcestershire sauce, garlic and hot sauce in a food processor or blender and process until smooth. Season with salt and pepper. Add the olive oil in a thin steady stream with the motor running and process until emulsified. Add the desired amount of dressing to the salad and toss to combine. Sprinkle with the cheese and serve.

Makes 6 servings

Sourdough Croutons

2 tablespoons olive oil
6 cups (3/4-inch) cubes sourdough bread (about 6 ounces)
6 tablespoons freshly grated Parmesan cheese
1/2 teaspoon garlic powder

Drizzle the olive oil over the bread cubes in a large bowl and toss to combine. Add the cheese and garlic powder and mix well. Spread the cubes on a large baking sheet. Bake at 350 degrees for 15 minutes or until golden brown, turning the cubes occasionally. Cool completely. Store in an airtight container at room temperatue for up to 24 hours.

Makes 6 cups croutons

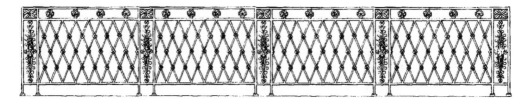

Jackson Salad

1/4 small onion
3 tablespoons cider vinegar
2 teaspoons spicy brown mustard
1/2 teaspoon sugar
1/2 teaspoon salt
1/4 teaspoon freshly ground pepper
3/4 to 1 cup canola oil or other vegetable oil
8 ounces bacon, crisp-cooked and crumbled
2 heads romaine, torn into bite-size pieces
1 (7-ounce) can hearts of palm, drained and sliced
1 (8-ounce) can water-pack artichoke hearts, drained and quartered
4 ounces blue cheese, crumbled

Combine the onion, vinegar, spicy brown mustard, sugar, salt and pepper in a food processor or blender and process for 10 to 20 seconds or until smooth. Add the canola oil in a thin steady stream with the motor running and process until emulsified. Combine the bacon, romaine, hearts of palm, artichoke hearts and blue cheese in a large salad bowl. Add the desired amount of dressing and toss to combine. Serve immediately.

Makes 6 to 8 servings

"Cooking is an art, but you eat it too."
—*Marcella Hazan*

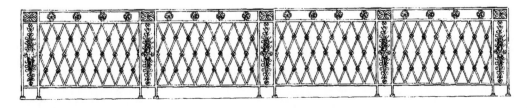

Crunchy Romaine Salad

1 cup walnuts, chopped
1 package ramen noodles, broken into pieces
  (discard the flavor packet)
1/4 cup (1/2 stick) unsalted butter
1 bunch broccoli, coarsely chopped
1 head romaine, torn into pieces
4 green onions, chopped
1 cup Sweet-and-Sour Dressing (below)

Brown the walnuts and noodles in the butter in a skillet. Cool on paper towels. Combine the walnuts, noodles, broccoli, romaine and green onions in a salad bowl. Add the Sweet-and-Sour Dressing and toss to combine.

Makes 10 to 12 servings

Sweet-and-Sour Dressing

1 cup vegetable oil
1 cup sugar
1/3 cup wine vinegar
1 tablespoon soy sauce
Salt and pepper to taste

Combine the oil, sugar, vinegar, soy sauce, salt and pepper in a blender and process until combined. Remove to a jar and shake well. Store in an airtight container in the refrigerator for up to 1 week.

Makes about 2 cups

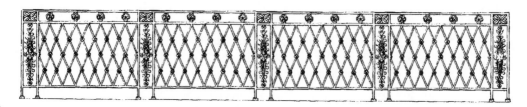

Salad with Warm Goat Cheese

The dressing:
2 tablespoons cider vinegar
2 tablespoons champagne vinegar
Pinch of sugar
1/2 teaspoon kosher salt, or to taste
1 extra-large egg yolk, or 1 tablespoon mayonnaise
1 cup olive oil

The salad:
2 extra-large egg whites
1 tablespoon water
1 (11-ounce) log plain goat cheese, sliced into
   12 (1/2-inch-thick) pieces (use dental floss)
Fresh white bread crumbs (trim bread crusts and
   process in a food processor for 15 seconds)
Mixed salad greens
1 tablespoon olive oil
1 tablespoon unsalted butter

For the dressing, combine the cider vinegar, champagne vinegar, sugar, salt and egg yolk in a food processor fitted with a steel blade and process for 1 minute. Add the olive oil in a thin steady stream with the motor running and process until emulsified. Adjust the seasonings to taste.

For the salad, beat the egg whites with 1 tablespoon water in a shallow dish. Dip each slice of goat cheese in the egg whites. Coat thoroughly with the bread crumbs. Place on a wire rack. Chill for at least 15 minutes. Arrange salad greens on 6 individual plates. Top with enough of the dressing to moisten. Heat the olive oil and butter in a skillet over medium-high heat. Sauté the goat cheese rounds quickly on both sides until brown on the outside but not melted on the inside. Place 2 warm cheese rounds on each salad.

Makes 6 servings

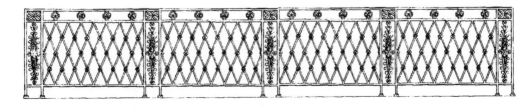

Corn Bread Salad

1 (8-ounce) package white corn bread mix
3 cups chopped tomatoes
1/2 to 1 cup chopped green bell pepper
1 cup chopped Vidalia onion or other sweet onion
1/2 cup chopped sweet pickles
12 slices bacon, crisp-cooked and crumbled
1 cup mayonnaise
1/4 cup sweet pickle juice

Prepare and bake the corn bread mix using the package directions. Let cool. Crumble 1/2 of the corn bread into a large salad bowl. Combine the tomatoes, bell pepper, onion, pickles and bacon in another bowl. Combine the mayonnaise and pickle juice in a small bowl. Layer the tomato mixture and mayonnaise mixture 1/2 at a time over the corn bread. Repeat the layers using the remaining corn bread, tomato mixture and mayonnaise mixture. Garnish as desired. Chill, tightly covered, for 2 to 3 hours before serving.

Makes 8 servings

Note: This recipe is from the Cornbread Festival in Pittsburg, Tennessee.

"I don't like gourmet cooking or 'this' cooking or
'that' cooking. I like 'good cooking.'"
—*James Beard* (1903–1985)

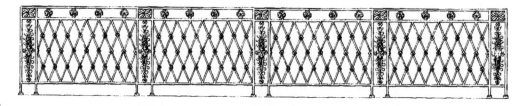

Panzanella (Tomato Bread Salad)

The vinaigrette:
1/2 cup basil chile garlic vinegar
2 tablespoons balsamic vinegar
6 garlic cloves, minced
2 teaspoons Dijon mustard
2 teaspoons fresh rosemary, minced
1 teaspoon thyme
2 or 3 minced anchovy fillets (optional)
Crushed red pepper to taste (optional)
3/4 cup olive oil
Salt and freshly ground pepper
  to taste

The salad:
1 loaf day-old crusty rustic bread,
  cut into 1-inch cubes

1 pound cherry tomatoes,
  halved and lightly salted
1 pound golden pear tomatoes,
  halved and lightly salted
1 head red-tipped lettuce, torn
4 cups field greens
2 cups arugula, stems trimmed
1 1/2 cups chopped roasted red and
  yellow bell peppers
2 cups chopped fresh basil
1/2 cup chopped Italian parsley
1 red onion, thinly sliced
1 bunch green onions, chopped
  (include some of the green tops)
3/4 cup kalamata olives
3 tablespoons capers

For the vinaigrette, combine the basil chile garlic vinegar, balsamic vinegar, garlic, Dijon mustard, rosemary, thyme, anchovy fillets and crushed red pepper in a bowl and mix well. Whisk in the olive oil a little at a time until well combined. Season with salt and pepper.

For the salad, toast the bread cubes at 350 degrees for 20 minutes or until barely crisp. Remove the bread to a large bowl. Drizzle with enough of the vinaigrette to moisten evenly. Add the cherry tomatoes and pear tomatoes and a little more of the vinaigrette and mix well. Let stand for 20 minutes or until the bread is softened but not mushy. Line a large serving platter with the red-tipped lettuce. Toss the field greens and arugula with a little of the vinaigrette. Add the bell peppers, basil, parsley, red onion, green onions, olives and capers to the bread mixture and mix well. Mound on top of the greens. Serve immediately with freshly grated Parmesan cheese, anchovies and capers.

Makes 10 to 12 servings

Note: The recipe is from *The Herb Cookbook* by Lucinda Hutson. It's a perfect summertime dish when tomatoes are at their best and fresh herbs are plentiful. For a southern twist, use corn bread instead of the rustic bread.

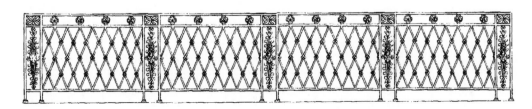

Frozen Tomato Salad with Horseradish Dressing

1 envelope unflavored gelatin	1 teaspoon Worcestershire sauce
1/3 cup cold water	2 drops of Tabasco sauce
1 (20-ounce) can tomatoes, drained	1 teaspoon salt
1 1/2 cups mayonnaise	Dash of cracked pepper
Juice of 1 1/2 lemons	Watercress
1 tablespoon finely chopped green onions	Horseradish Dressing (below)
	2 teaspoons chopped chives

Dissolve the gelatin in the water in a small bowl. Combine the tomatoes, mayonnaise, lemon juice, green onions, Worcestershire sauce, Tabasco sauce, salt, pepper and dissolved gelatin in a blender and process until smooth. Pour into a freezer container and freeze until firm, stirring several times. Scoop individual servings with an ice cream scoop and refreeze. Serve each scoop on a bed of watercress. Top with Horseradish Dressing and sprinkle with the chives.

Makes 6 to 8 servings

Horseradish Dressing

1 cup mayonnaise	2 garlic cloves, minced
1/2 cup sour cream	1/4 teaspoon dry mustard
4 teaspoons undrained horseradish	

Combine the mayonnaise, sour cream, horseradish, garlic and dry mustard in a blender and process until smooth.

Makes about 1 1/2 cups

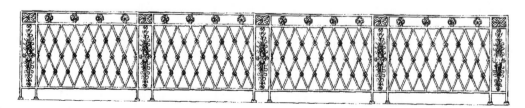

Zesty Pasta Salad

3 ounces tri-color rotini
1¹/2 cups (6 ounces) cubed or shredded mozzarella cheese
1 cup sliced mushrooms
³/4 cup canned tomatoes with juice
¹/2 cup sliced green bell pepper
¹/2 cup chopped onion
¹/4 cup Italian salad dressing
2 tablespoons grated Parmesan cheese

Cook the pasta using the package directions, omitting the salt; drain and rinse with cool water. Combine the pasta, mozzarella cheese, mushrooms, tomatoes, bell pepper and onion in a salad bowl. Add the salad dressing and toss to combine. Sprinkle with the Parmesan cheese just before serving.

Makes 4 to 6 servings

"Never eat more than you can lift!"
—*Miss Piggy*

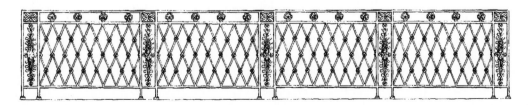

Marinated Salad

1 (15-ounce) can white asparagus spears, drained
1 (14-ounce) can artichoke hearts, drained and cut in half
1 (14-ounce) can hearts of palm, drained and
   cut into $1/2$-inch pieces
1 (14-ounce) can sliced mushrooms, drained
$1/2$ cup black olives, sliced
$1/2$ cup pimento-stuffed olives, sliced
12 cherry tomatoes, cut into halves
$1/2$ red onion, sliced and separated into rings
1 (8-ounce) bottle Italian salad dressing
Romaine

Combine the asparagus, artichoke hearts, hearts of palm, mushrooms, black olives, pimento-stuffed olives, tomatoes, onion and salad dressing in a salad bowl and toss gently. Marinate in the refrigerator for at least 30 minutes. Drain the salad and serve on a bed of romaine.

Makes 6 servings

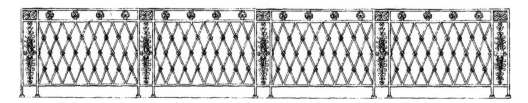

Broccoli Cauliflower Salad

1 bunch broccoli, stems removed and
  florets cut into small pieces
1 head cauliflower, cut into small florets
1 pound bacon, crisp-cooked and crumbled
8 ounces shredded Cheddar cheese
1/2 red onion, diced
1 1/2 ounces shelled sunflower seeds
1 cup mayonnaise
1/2 cup sugar
2 tablespoons vinegar

Combine the broccoli, cauliflower, bacon, cheese, onion and sunflower seeds
in a salad bowl. Whisk the mayonnaise, sugar and vinegar together in a small
bowl. Pour over the salad and toss to combine.

Makes 6 to 8 servings

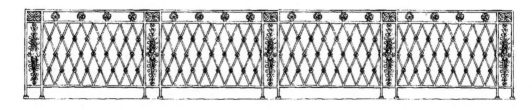

Apple, Endive and Gorgonzola Salad

The dressing:
4 teaspoons cider vinegar
1 teaspoon balsamic vinegar
1 teaspoon honey
1/4 cup extra-virgin olive oil
Salt and pepper to taste

The salad:
1/4 cup walnuts
3 Belgian endive
1 Granny Smith apple
1/2 cup (2 ounces) crumbled Gorgonzola cheese
1 teaspoon minced fresh chives
Salt and pepper to taste
4 teaspoons honey

For the dressing, whisk the cider vinegar, balsamic vinegar and honey together in a small bowl. Add the olive oil in a thin stream, whisking until emulsified. Season with salt and pepper.

For the salad, toast the walnuts in a shallow baking pan at 350 degrees for 10 minutes or until fragrant. Let cool and chop. Separate 4 outer leaves from each endive. Arrange 3 leaves on each of 4 salad plates. Cut the remaining endive crosswise into 1/4-inch slices. Toss with the dressing and divide among the salad plates, mounding in the whole endive leaves. Peel the apple and cut thin slices lengthwise from the 4 sides, stopping just before the core. Make small stacks of the slices and cut the stacks into julienne strips. Top the endive with the apple, walnuts, cheese, chives, salt and pepper. Drizzle 1 teaspoon honey over each plate.

Makes 4 servings

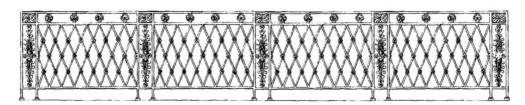

Mandarin Orange Salad

The dressing:
1/4 cup vegetable oil
2 tablespoons vinegar
2 tablespoons sugar
1/2 teaspoon salt
1/8 teaspoon almond extract
Dash of pepper

The salad:
1 tablespoon margarine
1/4 cup slivered almonds
2 tablespoons sugar
1 cup diced celery
3/4 head lettuce
2 green onions, chopped
1 can mandarin oranges, drained and chilled

For the dressing, combine the oil, vinegar, sugar, salt, almond extract and pepper in a jar and shake well.

For the salad, heat the margarine in a small skillet. Add the almonds and sugar. Cook until the almonds are brown, stirring constantly. Cool on a sheet of foil; break into small pieces. Combine the almonds, celery, lettuce and onions in a salad bowl. Chill until serving time. Add the mandarin oranges and dressing and toss gently to combine.

Makes 10 servings

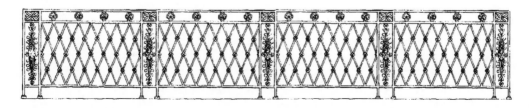

Ambrosia

1 coconut, cracked and grated, or
   1 package flaked coconut
4 navel oranges, sectioned
2 cups pineapple chunks
Sugar to taste

Layer a little each of the coconut, orange sections and pineapple chunks in a glass bowl. Sprinkle with a little sugar. Repeat until all the ingredients are used. Chill for 8 to 10 hours before serving.

Makes 6 to 8 servings

Note: Many a southern grandmother served a crystal bowl of ambrosia at the Christmas lunch table. It was often served as a side dish with the meal rather than as a dessert.

Apricot Gelatin Salad

1 (3-ounce) package apricot gelatin
$3/4$ cup sugar
1 (8-ounce) can crushed pineapple
8 ounces cream cheese, softened
1 (7-ounce) jar junior baby food apricot tapioca pudding
8 ounces whipped topping

Combine the gelatin, sugar and pineapple in a saucepan. Bring to a boil, stirring constantly. Let cool. Combine the cream cheese and pudding in a large bowl and mix well. Add the gelatin mixture and stir well. Fold in the whipped topping. Pour into a mold. Chill until firm.

Makes 9 servings

Note: Double the recipe and mold in a 9×13-inch baking dish to serve 12 to 15.

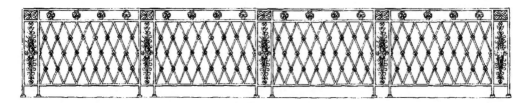

Autumn Salad

1 (3-ounce) package orange gelatin
1 (3-ounce) package lemon gelatin or apricot gelatin
1 cup boiling water
1 small can crushed pineapple
2 small cans mandarin oranges
1/2 cup dried cranberries
1/2 cup chopped nuts
1 (8-ounce) package miniature marshmallows
1 cup heavy cream or whipping cream
1 tablespoon sugar
1/2 cup mayonnaise
1/4 cup shredded Cheddar cheese

Dissolve the orange gelatin and lemon gelatin in the hot water in a large bowl. Drain the pineapple and mandarin oranges, reserving the juice from both. Combine the juice and enough water to measure 3 cups. Stir into the dissolved gelatin. Add the pineapple, oranges, cranberries, nuts and marshmallows and stir well. Pour into a 9×11-inch baking dish. Chill until partially set. Whip the cream and sugar in a mixing bowl until firm peaks form. Fold in the mayonnaise. Spread evenly over the gelatin salad. Sprinkle with the cheese. Chill until firm.

Makes 8 to 10 servings

Note: This gelatin salad is especially easy because it doesn't require waiting for different stages of congealing. It goes well with chicken tetrazzini and broccoli salad.

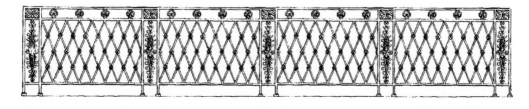

cranberry salad

1 (3-ounce) package cherry or strawberry gelatin
1 cup hot water
1/2 cup cold water
8 ounces cranberries, coarsely ground
3 apples (such as Granny Smith), peeled and chopped
2 oranges, sectioned and chopped, or
   1/2 cup crushed pineapple, drained
1/4 cup nuts, chopped
3/4 cup sugar
4 cups salad greens (optional)

Dissolve the gelatin in the hot water in a bowl. Add the cold water. Chill until partially set. Combine the cranberries, apples, oranges, nuts and sugar in a bowl and mix well. Fold into the partially set gelatin. Pour into a mold. Chill until firm. Unmold onto a plate lined with the salad greens.

Makes 8 to 10 servings

Note: Purchase several bags of fresh cranberries when they are in season and store them in your freezer. You can enjoy this salad all year long.

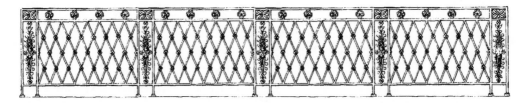

Poppy Seed Dressing

2/3 cup vegetable oil
1/2 cup sugar
1/4 cup vinegar
1 tablespoon poppy seeds
1 teaspoon prepared mustard
1 teaspoon salt

Combine the oil, sugar, vinegar, poppy seeds, mustard and salt in a jar with a tight-fitting lid and shake well. Store in the refrigerator. Serve over fruit.

Makes 1 cup

Note: This dressing is easily made from a few ingredients and keeps well in the refrigerator for a long time.

Amazing Vinaigrette

1/2 cup olive oil
1/4 cup red wine vinegar
1 tablespoon Creole mustard or Dijon mustard
1 teaspoon sugar
1/2 teaspoon salt
1/2 teaspoon pepper

Combine the olive oil, vinegar, Creole mustard, sugar, salt and pepper in a jar with a tight-fitting lid and shake well. Store in the refrigerator for up to 2 weeks.

Makes about 1 1/4 cups

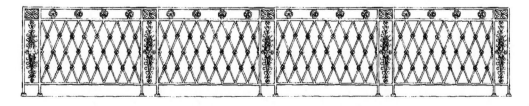

Basic Vinaigrette Dressing

1 cup extra-virgin olive oil
1/2 cup balsamic or herbed vinegar
  (may use part balsamic or any herbed vinegar)
2 teaspoons Dijon mustard, or 1/4 teaspoon dry mustard
1 teaspoon sugar
1/2 teaspoon salt
1/4 teaspoon pepper
1 teaspoon dried herbs, or 1 tablespoon fresh chopped herbs
  (such as dill weed, basil, lemon basil or lemon thyme)

Combine the olive oil, vinegar, Dijon mustard, sugar, salt, pepper and herbs in a jar with a tight-fitting lid and shake well.

Makes 1 1/2 cups

Mandarin Orange Vinaigrette

1 (8-ounce) can mandarin oranges, drained
1/4 cup red wine vinegar
1 tablespoon honey
1/4 teaspoon salt
1/4 teaspoon pepper
2/3 cup vegetable oil

Combine the oranges, vinegar, honey, salt and pepper in a blender or food processor and turn on the motor. Add the oil in a thin stream and process until emulsified. Serve at once or store in the refrigerator for up to 2 weeks. Serve over plain salad greens.

Makes about 1 1/2 cups

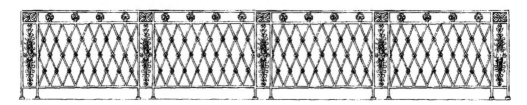

Main Dishes

"The pleasantest hours of our life are all connected....
with some memory of the table."

Charles Pierre Monselet

Filet Mignon with Rich Balsamic Glaze

2 (4- to 6-ounce) beef tenderloin steaks
Salt to taste
1/2 teaspoon freshly ground pepper
1/4 cup balsamic vinegar
1/4 cup dry red wine

Season the steaks with the salt and pepper. Heat a nonstick skillet over medium-high heat. Cook the steaks in the heated skillet for 1 minute on each side or until brown. Reduce the heat to medium-low. Stir in the vinegar and wine. Cook, covered, for 4 minutes on each side, basting with the sauce when the meat is turned. Remove the steaks to warmed plates and spoon 1 tablespoon of the glaze over each steak.

Makes 2 servings

Note: If you like your filet medium, you may need to cook it a little longer. The glaze will become even more caramelized and tastes great.

"Serve this dish with much too much wine for your guests,
along with some cooked green vegetables and a huge salad.
You will be famous in about half an hour."
—*Jeff Smith,* The Frugal Gourmet

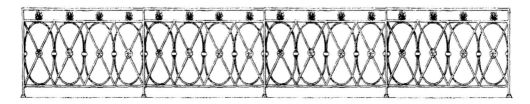

Beef Wellington

The pastry:
4 cups all-purpose flour
1 teaspoon salt
1¼ cups (2½ sticks) butter
6 tablespoons ice water

The duxelles sauce:
2 to 3 cans mushrooms, drained
  and finely chopped
¼ cup (½ stick) butter or margarine
Green onions, finely chopped
½ cup cooked ground ham or
  chicken livers

2 tablespoons chopped
  fresh parsley
½ tablespoon all-purpose flour
½ cup beef broth
2 tablespoons sherry

The tenderloin:
4 pounds beef tenderloin, tied
2 tablespoons butter, softened
Salt and pepper to taste
1 egg, beaten
1 tablespoon water

For the pastry, combine the flour and salt in a bowl. Cut in the butter until crumbly. Add the ice water 1 tablespoon at a time, mixing with a fork until the mixture forms a ball. Chill, wrapped in plastic wrap, for 30 minutes or longer.

For the duxelles sauce, sauté the mushrooms in the butter in a skillet until the liquid is evaporated. Add the green onions, ham and parsley. Cook for 5 minutes longer. Stir in the flour, broth and sherry. Cook until thickened, stirring constantly. Cool completely.

For the tenderloin, rub the beef with the butter and season with salt and pepper. Bake at 425 degrees for 30 minutes. Let stand until cool. Remove the strings. Proceed with the recipe or store in the refrigerator for 1 to 3 days. Roll the pastry into an 8×12-inch rectangle on a lightly floured surface. Spread the duxelles sauce over the pastry, leaving a 1-inch edge. Place the tenderloin in the center of the pastry. Roll to enclose the tenderloin, sealing the edge and ends. Wrap in plastic wrap and chill in the refrigerator until 1 hour before baking. Beat the egg with the water in a small bowl. Brush over the pastry. Bake at 425 degrees for 30 minutes.

Makes 10 to 12 servings

Note: This dish will always get compliments. Serve it at special holidays and to special people.

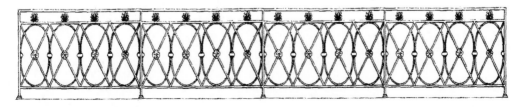

Greek Shish Kabob

2 pounds stew beef, beef tenderloin or lamb,
  cut into cubes
2 garlic cloves, chopped
2 teaspoons oregano
2 teaspoons salt
1 teaspoon pepper
1 teaspoon sugar
$1/4$ cup olive oil
$1/4$ cup red wine vinegar
1 large onion, cut into small chunks
Mushrooms
1 or 2 bell peppers (any color), cut into small chunks
2 tablespoons olive oil
Salt and pepper to taste
Lemon juice

Place the meat in a shallow dish. Combine the garlic, oregano, 2 teaspoons salt, 1 teaspoon pepper and the sugar in a small bowl. Whisk $1/4$ cup olive oil with the vinegar in a bowl. Add to the garlic mixture and mix well. Pour over the meat. Marinate, covered, in the refrigerator for 8 to 10 hours. Combine the onion, mushrooms and bell pepper in a shallow roasting pan. Add 2 tablespoons olive oil and salt and pepper to taste and mix well. Bake at 350 degrees for 5 to 10 minutes or until the vegetables are almost tender. Alternate the beef and vegetables on skewers. Squeeze lemon juice over the skewers. Grill over hot coals to desired doneness.

Makes 5 to 6 servings

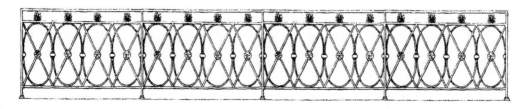

Company Corned Beef

4 to 5 pounds corned beef
1 small onion, sliced
1 rib celery, cut into chunks
2 bay leaves
5 peppercorns
2 sprigs parsley
Whole cloves
2 tablespoons butter or margarine
1/3 cup packed brown sugar
1/3 cup ketchup
1 tablespoon prepared mustard
3 tablespoons vinegar
3 tablespoons water

Wash the corned beef thoroughly to remove the brine. Place in a large kettle and cover with cold water. Add the onion, celery, bay leaves, peppercorns and parsley. Bring to a boil. Reduce the heat and simmer, covered, for 3 to 3³/4 hours (about 45 minutes per pound) or until tender. Remove the corned beef to a shallow baking dish. Stud with whole cloves. Melt the butter in a small saucepan. Stir in the brown sugar, ketchup, mustard, vinegar and water. Cook over medium heat until smooth. Pour over the corned beef. Bake at 350 degrees for 30 minutes, basting often with the sauce. Serve hot or cold.

Makes 10 to 12 servings

Note: When guests taste this, compliments come quickly.

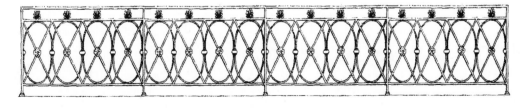

Little Meat Loaves

1 pound lean ground beef
1 pound bulk pork sausage
2 eggs, lightly beaten
3/4 cup crushed butter crackers
1/2 cup chopped onion
1/2 cup milk
1/2 cup (2 ounces) grated Parmesan cheese
1 teaspoon Italian seasoning
1 teaspoon minced garlic
1 teaspoon Worcestershire sauce
1 cup ketchup
1/2 cup packed brown sugar
1 tablespoon Worcestershire sauce

Combine the ground beef, sausage, eggs, cracker crumbs, onion, milk, cheese, Italian seasoning, garlic and 1 teaspoon Worcestershire sauce in a large bowl and mix well. Shape into 6 individual loaves. Place in a 9×13-inch baking dish. Combine the ketchup, brown sugar and 1 tablespoon Worcestershire sauce in a small bowl and mix well. Spoon evenly over the loaves. Bake at 350 degrees for 45 to 60 minutes.

Makes 6 servings

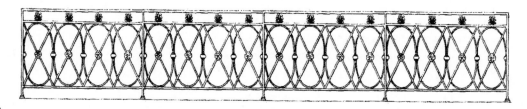

Bolognese Sauce for Spaghetti

4 slices bacon, cut into small pieces
3 tablespoons butter
1 onion, chopped
1 carrot, chopped
1 rib celery, chopped
2 tablespoons olive oil
$1/3$ pound ground veal
$1/3$ pound ground pork
$1/3$ pound ground round
1 cup white wine
2 cups beef broth
3 tablespoons tomato paste
Salt and pepper to taste
1 cup heavy cream or whipping cream
Hot cooked pasta
Grated Parmesan cheese

Sauté the bacon in the butter in a large saucepan until brown; drain, reserving the drippings in the pan. Add the onion, carrot and celery to the drippings. Cook, uncovered, for about 10 minutes. Remove the vegetables to a bowl. Add the olive oil to the pan. Brown the veal, pork and ground round in the olive oil, stirring until crumbly. Remove the meat from the pan and drain well. Return the meat to the pan. Add the wine. Cook until most of the wine is evaporated, stirring constantly. Stir in the bacon, vegetables, broth, tomato paste, salt and pepper. Simmer, partially covered, for 40 to 60 minutes or until the sauce is reduced and thickened, stirring occasionally. Add the cream. Cook just until heated through; do not boil. Serve over pasta and top with grated Parmesan cheese.

Makes 6 servings

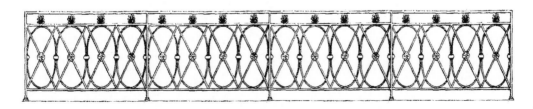

Spaghetti Sauce

1 1/2 pounds ground sirloin
1 white onion, chopped
1 large green bell pepper, chopped
8 ounces fresh mushrooms, sliced
2 (15-ounce) cans tomato sauce
2 (6-ounce) cans tomato paste
1 bottle chili sauce
1/4 cup soy sauce
1 teaspoon oregano
1 teaspoon Italian seasoning
1 teaspoon curry powder
1/2 teaspoon crushed red pepper
1/2 teaspoon paprika
1/2 teaspoon garlic powder
Salt and pepper to taste
Hot cooked spaghetti
Grated Parmesan cheese

Cook the ground sirloin, onion and bell pepper in a skillet until the ground sirloin is crumbly and the vegetables are tender; drain. Add the mushrooms, tomato sauce, tomato paste, chili sauce, soy sauce, oregano, Italian seasoning, curry powder, crushed red pepper, paprika and garlic powder and mix well. Bring to a boil. Reduce the heat and simmer, covered, for 2 hours, stirring occasionally and adding water if the sauce is too thick. Season with salt and pepper. Serve over spaghetti and sprinkle with Parmesan cheese.

Makes 8 to 10 servings

Note: If you want a new twist on a traditional spaghetti sauce, try this recipe.

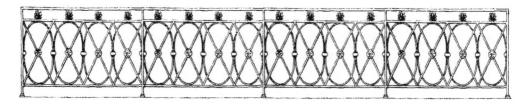

Spaghetti and Meatballs

1 1/2 pounds ground round
15 saltines, crushed into fine crumbs
1 onion, finely chopped
1 egg
2 teaspoons Italian seasoning
2 (28-ounce) cans crushed tomatoes
1 (28-ounce) can tomato sauce
1 (6-ounce) can tomato paste
2 tablespoons sugar
2 teaspoons Italian seasoning
Hot cooked angel hair pasta
Freshly grated Parmesan cheese

Combine the ground round, cracker crumbs, onion, egg and 2 teaspoons Italian seasoning in a bowl and mix gently with clean hands. Shape into meatballs of desired size. Brown lightly on all sides in a skillet coated with nonstick cooking spray. Combine the crushed tomatoes, tomato sauce, tomato paste, sugar and 2 teaspoons Italian seasoning in a Dutch oven. Bring to a boil. Reduce the heat to low and add the meatballs. Simmer for 2 to 4 hours, stirring occasionally. Serve over angel hair pasta with Parmesan cheese.

Makes 8 servings

Note: The longer this sauce cooks, the more flavor it will have. You can use a heat diffuser to keep the sauce from sticking.

Roast Veal Dijon

1 small rolled boned leg of veal
1/2 cup (1 stick) butter, melted
1 (8-ounce) jar wine-flavored Dijon mustard
1 (10-ounce) can consommé
1/4 cup sherry
Arrowroot or flour
Chopped fresh parsley

Place the veal in a shallow roasting pan. Combine the butter and Dijon mustard in a small bowl and mix well. Pour over the veal, covering all sides. Roast at 300 degrees for 4 hours, basting every 20 minutes during the last hour with a mixture of the consommé and sherry. Let stand, loosely covered with foil, for 20 to 30 minutes before carving. Thicken the pan juices with arrowroot or flour. Remove to a gravy boat and sprinkle with parsley. Slice the veal and serve with the gravy.

Makes 2 to 4 servings

Rack of Lamb

1/2 cup soy sauce
1 cup good-quality merlot
4 garlic cloves, minced
2 tablespoons dried oregano
1 tablespoon dried rosemary
1 tablespoon pepper
2 racks of lamb

Combine the soy sauce, merlot, garlic, oregano, rosemary and pepper in a sealable plastic bag. Add the lamb. Marinate in the refrigerator for at least 6 hours, turning the bag occasionally. Remove the lamb from the marinade, discarding the marinade. Roast in a shallow roasting pan at 475 degrees for 10 minutes. Reduce the heat to 375 degrees. Roast for 10 minutes longer for medium-rare meat. Let stand for 10 minutes. Cut into serving-size portions.

Makes 6 to 8 servings

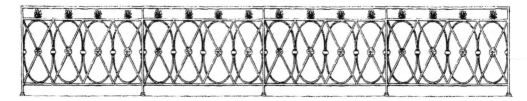

Herb- and Bread-Crusted Rack of Lamb

The coating:
1/2 cup fresh bread crumbs
2 tablespoons chopped fresh rosemary, savory, thyme or oregano
2 teaspoons minced garlic
1 teaspoon salt
1/4 teaspoon freshly ground pepper
2 tablespoons olive oil

The lamb:
1 (7- or 8-bone) rack of lamb, trimmed and frenched
Salt and freshly ground pepper to taste
1 to 2 tablespoons olive oil
2 tablespoons Dijon mustard

For the coating, combine the bread crumbs, rosemary, garlic, salt and pepper in a bowl. Add the olive oil and mix well. Spread in a shallow baking dish.

For the lamb, season the lamb with salt and pepper. Heat the olive oil in a heavy 10-inch ovenproof skillet over high heat. Sear the lamb in the skillet for 1 to 2 minutes on each side. Let the lamb stand, uncovered, for a few minutes. Brush with the Dijon mustard. Coat with the bread crumb mixture, pressing the crumbs into the lamb. Place the lamb in the skillet bone side down. Cover the ends of the chops with foil to prevent burning. Roast on the middle rack of the oven at 475 degrees for 15 to 20 minutes or to the desired degree of doneness, checking after the first 12 to 15 minutes. Broil for 1 to 2 minutes to make the coating crispier, if desired. Let stand, loosely covered with foil, for 5 to 7 minutes before carving. Cut between the ribs, serving 3 to 4 chops per person.

Makes 2 to 3 servings

Note: Use an instant-read thermometer to determine the doneness of your lamb. Here is a temperature guide: Blood-rare: 115 to 125 degrees; Rare: 125 to 130 degrees; Medium-rare: 130 to 140 degrees.

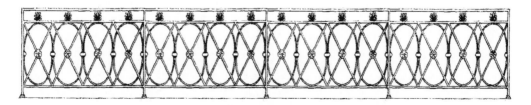

Roasted Pork Loin with Green Peppercorn Sauce

1 bone-in pork loin roast (about 7 pounds), frenched and tied
2 tablespoons extra-virgin olive oil
1 teaspoon ground fennel seeds
1 tablespoon salt, or to taste
1 1/2 cups unsalted chicken stock
1 bay leaf
1 tablespoon all-purpose flour
1/2 cup white wine
1 teaspoon Dijon mustard
2 tablespoons green peppercorns, rinsed

Let the pork stand at room temperature for 30 minutes. Rub with the olive oil. Season with the fennel seeds and salt. Set the pork on a rack in a large roasting pan. Roast at 400 degrees for 1 1/4 to 1 1/4 hours, or until the internal temperature reaches 140 degrees on a meat thermometer for medium. Remove to a cutting board. Let stand, loosely covered with foil. Bring the stock and bay leaf to a simmer in a small saucepan over medium-high heat. Cool for 30 minutes; remove and discard the bay leaf. Remove all but 2 tablespoons of the drippings from the roasting pan. Heat the pan over medium heat. Add the flour and stir, scraping up any brown bits in the pan. Whisk in the cooled stock, wine, Dijon mustard and peppercorns. Cook for 2 to 3 minutes or until the sauce is slightly thickened. Add salt if necessary. Remove to a sauceboat. Slice the roast between the bones and serve with the sauce.

Make 6 to 8 servings

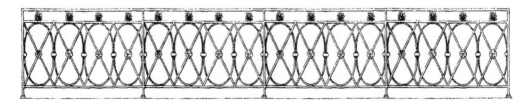

Six-Hour Pork Roast

10 garlic cloves
2 tablespoons finely chopped fresh sage
2 tablespoons fresh rosemary
1 tablespoon fennel seeds
1 1/2 tablespoons coarse salt
1 tablespoon cracked pepper
1 tablespoon dry white wine
1 tablespoon olive oil
1 (6-pound) boneless pork Boston shoulder roast

Combine the garlic, sage, rosemary, fennel seeds, salt and pepper in a food processor and process until a thick paste forms. Add the wine and olive oil and process until well combined. Trim the roast, leaving a 1/8-inch layer of fat. Make 3 incisions 1 inch long and 1 inch deep in each side of the pork with a small sharp knife. Fill each incision with about 1 teaspoon of the herb paste. Spread the remaining paste over the roast. Tie with kitchen string at 2-inch intervals. Place the pork fat side up in a roasting pan. Roast on the middle rack of the oven at 275 degrees for 6 hours. Remove to a cutting board. Let stand for 15 minutes. Remove and discard the string. Cut the roast into thick slices.

Makes 6 servings

Note: Make the herb paste a day ahead and chill, covered, until you are ready to roast the pork.

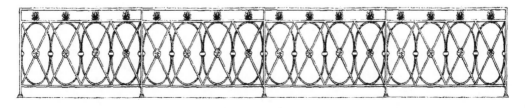

Sweet-and-Sour Pork Chops

6 (3/4-inch-thick) pork chops, trimmed
1 large onion, sliced
1 garlic clove, minced
1 cup pineapple juice
1 (8-ounce) can tomato sauce
1/4 cup packed brown sugar
2 tablespoons lemon juice
1 teaspoon salt
3 cups hot cooked rice
2 tablespoons all-purpose flour

Brown the pork chops slowly in their own fat in a skillet; drain, reserving
2 tablespoons of the drippings. Arrange the pork chops in a single layer in
a shallow baking pan. Sauté the onion and garlic in the reserved drippings in
the skillet until tender. Stir in the pineapple juice, tomato sauce, brown sugar,
lemon juice and salt. Bring to a boil, stirring constantly. Simmer for 5 minutes.
Pour over the pork chops. Bake, covered, at 350 degrees for 45 minutes or
until tender. Spoon the rice onto a serving platter. Arrange the pork chops
and onion over the rice. Skim the fat from the pan juices. Bring the juices to
a boil. Whisk in the flour and cook until thickened, stirring constantly. Spoon
over the pork chops.

Makes 6 servings

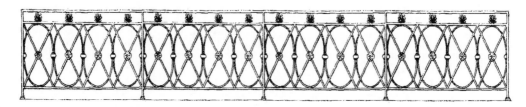

Ham Rolls with Savory Sauce

16 thin ham slices
16 slices Swiss cheese
2 (10-ounce) packages frozen broccoli spears, thawed
1 (10-ounce) can cream of chicken soup
1/4 cup (1/2 stick) butter, melted
1/3 cup half-and-half
1/4 cup lemon juice
Salt and pepper to taste

Top each ham slice with a slice of cheese. Place 2 broccoli spears with
the florets facing in opposite direction on each cheese slice. Roll to enclose
the broccoli. Place ham rolls seam side down in a buttered 3-quart baking
dish. Combine the soup, butter, half-and-half, lemon juice, salt and pepper
in a bowl and mix well. Pour over the ham rolls. Bake at 350 degrees for
30 minutes. Serve with rice.

Makes 8 servings

Note: This may be made the day before. Don't pour the sauce over the ham
rolls until ready to bake. Asparagus can be substituted for the broccoli.

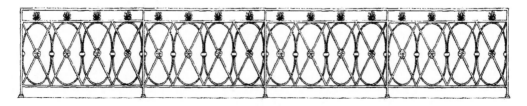

chicken Asparagus casserole

24 to 32 asparagus spears, cooked until
   tender-crisp and drained
8 chicken breasts, skinned, boned and cut into halves
1/4 cup (1/2 stick) butter
6 shallots, finely chopped
2 tablespoons (or more) butter
1/4 cup all-purpose flour
1 teaspoon salt
1/2 teaspoon pepper
1 1/2 cups light cream
1/2 cup dry white wine
1/2 cup (2 ounces) grated Parmesan cheese

Arrange the asparagus spears in a buttered shallow 2-quart baking dish.
Sauté the chicken in 1/4 cup butter in a skillet until cooked through. Layer
over the asparagus. Add the shallots and 2 tablespoons butter to the skillet,
adding additional butter as needed. Sauté until the shallots are tender. Whisk
in the flour, salt and pepper. Add the cream and wine gradually. Cook until
thickened, stirring constantly. Add 1/2 of the cheese and stir until melted. Pour
over the chicken. Sprinkle with the remaining cheese. Bake at 375 degrees
for 20 to 25 minutes or until warmed through.

Makes 6 servings

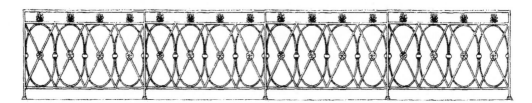

chicken Marbella

4 (2¹/₂-pound) chickens, quartered
1 head garlic, puréed
¹/₂ cup red wine vinegar
¹/₂ cup olive oil
1 cup pitted prunes
¹/₂ cup pitted Spanish green olives
¹/₂ cup capers with a little of the juice
¹/₄ cup dried oregano
6 bay leaves
Coarse salt and freshly ground pepper to taste
1 cup packed brown sugar
1 cup white wine
¹/₄ cup finely chopped fresh Italian parsley or cilantro

Combine the chicken, garlic, vinegar, olive oil, prunes, olives, capers, oregano, bay leaves, salt and pepper in a large bowl. Marinate, covered, in the refrigerator for 8 to 10 hours. Arrange the chicken in a single layer in a large shallow baking pan. Spoon the marinade evenly over the chicken. Sprinkle evenly with the brown sugar. Pour the wine around the chicken pieces. Bake at 350 degrees for 50 to 60 minutes or until the thigh juices run clear, basting frequently with the pan juices. Remove and discard the bay leaves. Remove the chicken, prunes, olives and capers with a slotted spoon to a serving platter. Moisten with a few spoonfuls of the pan juices. Sprinkle generously with the parsley. Pass the remaining pan juices in a sauceboat.

Makes 10 or more servings

Note: This recipe, taken from *The Silver Palate Cookbook,* is just as delicious served cold. Make it ahead and refrigerate, covered. Bring back to room temperature before serving.

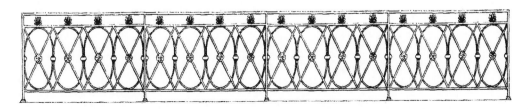

chicken Marengo

¹/4 cup all-purpose flour
¹/2 teaspoon salt
¹/4 teaspoon pepper
4 (6-ounce) boneless skinless chicken breasts
¹/4 cup extra-virgin olive oil
3 large portobello mushrooms, stems and
   gills discarded and caps thinly sliced
1 small shallot, finely chopped
1 garlic clove, minced
¹/2 teaspoon thyme, crumbled
¹/2 cup dry red wine
1 (15-ounce) can whole tomatoes, drained and chopped
¹/2 cup beef demi-glace or veal demi-glace
   (available at specialty food stores)
¹/2 cup water
Pepper to taste

Combine the flour, salt and ¹/4 teaspoon pepper in a sealable plastic bag. Add the chicken breasts 1 at a time and shake well. Remove and shake off excess flour. Sauté smooth side down in the olive oil in a 12-inch heavy ovenproof skillet for 2 minutes or until golden brown. Turn the chicken. Sauté for 1 minute longer. Scatter the mushrooms around the chicken. Bake, uncovered, at 350 degrees for 5 to 10 minutes or until just cooked through. Remove the chicken to a serving plate using a slotted spoon. Add the shallot, garlic and thyme to the skillet. Cook over medium-high heat for 1 minute, stirring constantly. Add the wine. Bring to a boil, stirring and scraping up the brown bits. Cook for 1 minute or until reduced by half. Add the tomatoes, demi-glace and water. Simmer for 4 minutes or until the mushrooms are tender and the sauce is reduced by half. Season with pepper to taste. Return the chicken to the skillet. Simmer for 1 minute or until heated through.

Makes 4 servings

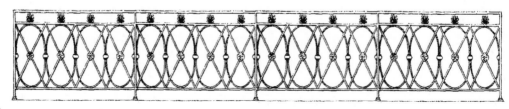

chicken and Dumplings

The chicken:
1 stewing hen, or 6 large chicken breasts
Chopped carrots
Chopped celery
Chopped onions
Salt and pepper to taste

The dumplings:
2 cups all-purpose flour
1 teaspoon salt
1/4 teaspoon pepper (optional)
1/4 cup canola oil
Milk

For the chicken, cook the chicken in water to cover in a stockpot for
1 hour or until the meat separates easily from the bones. Strain the stock into
another soup pot. Cut the chicken into large chunks, discarding the skin and
bones. Add the carrots, celery, onions, salt and pepper to the stock. Add
more water or canned chicken broth if necessary to increase the volume.
Cook until the vegetables are tender. Strain the stock, if desired.

For the dumplings, combine the flour, salt, and pepper in a bowl. Stir in the
canola oil and enough milk to make a soft dough. Knead lightly on a floured
surface. Roll into very thin sheets. Cut into small squares. Drop 1 at a time into
the boiling stock. Simmer for 30 minutes or until the dumplings are cooked.
Add the chicken.

Makes 6 to 8 servings

Note: This classic family favorite is great on a cold winter night served with a
pan of hot corn bread.

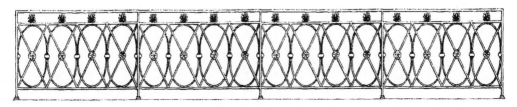

Gourmet Chicken Casserole

1 cup (2 sticks) butter
1 cup all-purpose flour
4 cups chicken broth (from cooking chicken)
1 cup half-and-half
1/2 cup sherry
2 teaspoons Worcestershire sauce
1 teaspoon salt
1/4 teaspoon ground red pepper
8 ounces fresh mushrooms, sliced
Butter
4 cups (1 pound) shredded sharp Cheddar cheese
4 cups chopped cooked chicken
4 cups chopped cooked shrimp
1 (14-ounce) can artichoke hearts, cut up
1 cup fine dry bread crumbs
Paprika

Melt 1 cup butter in a heavy saucepan. Whisk in the flour. Add the broth and half-and-half. Cook over medium heat until smooth and thickened, stirring constantly. Add more broth to thin if necessary. Add the sherry, Worcestershire sauce, salt and red pepper and stir until smooth. Sauté the mushrooms in a small amount of butter in a skillet until tender. Spread 1/3 of the sauce in a lightly greased 3-quart oblong casserole. Sprinkle with 1/2 of the cheese and spread with 1/2 of the remaining sauce. Top with the chicken, shrimp, mushrooms and artichoke hearts. Layer with the remaining cheese and sauce. Sprinkle with the bread crumbs and paprika. Bake at 350 degrees for 30 minutes or until bubbly.

Makes 12 to 15 servings

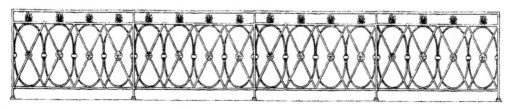

chicken Enchilada casserole

4 or 5 boneless skinless chicken breasts
Dried minced onion to taste
Salt and pepper to taste
1 (10-ounce) can cream of chicken soup
1 (10-ounce) can cream of mushroom soup
1/2 cup sour cream
1 onion, chopped
1 (4-ounce) can diced green chiles
1 (10-ounce) can tomatoes with green chiles, drained
12 corn tortillas
4 cups (1 pound) mixed shredded Cheddar and
  Monterey Jack cheese or Mexican blend cheese

Season the chicken breasts with dried minced onion, salt and pepper.
Bake, wrapped in foil, at 350 degrees for 1 hour. Cut into bite-size pieces,
reserving the juices in the foil. Combine the cream of chicken soup, cream
of mushroom soup, sour cream, onion, green chiles, tomatoes with green
chiles and a little of the cooking juices in a bowl and mix well. Stir in the
chicken pieces. Layer the tortillas, chicken mixture and cheese 1/2 at a time
in a greased casserole, ending with the cheese. Bake at 350 degrees for
30 to 45 minutes or until bubbly.

Makes 6 to 8 servings

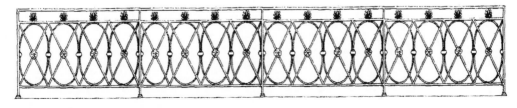

Mexican Chicken Casserole

2 tablespoons butter
1 package Mexican-style rice mix
1 green bell pepper, chopped
1 onion, chopped
2¹/4 cups water
2¹/4 cups cubed cooked chicken
1¹/2 (15-ounce) cans Mexican-style stewed tomatoes or
   chopped tomatoes
1¹/4 cups (5 ounces) shredded Mexican-style cheese or
   Cheddar cheese

Melt the butter in a large skillet. Add the rice mix, reserving the seasoning packet. Stir in the bell pepper and onion. Cook for several minutes or until the rice is brown, stirring constantly. Add the water and seasoning from the packet. Bring to a boil. Reduce the heat and simmer, covered, for 15 to 20 minutes or until the rice has absorbed all the water. Remove from the heat. Stir in the chicken, tomatoes and ¹/2 cup of the cheese. Pour into a greased casserole. Bake, uncovered, at 350 degrees for 20 minutes. Sprinkle with the remaining cheese. Bake for 5 to 10 minutes longer or until the cheese is melted and the casserole is heated through.

Makes 4 to 6 servings

Note: Serve with corn tortillas cut into strips, baked for 5 to 6 minutes, and sprinkled with a little salt. Add a green salad and you have a meal.

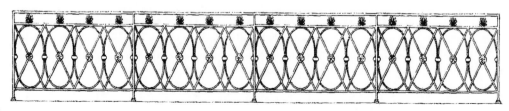

chicken Florentine with Sherry Artichoke Sauce

2 garlic cloves, minced
2 tablespoons butter
8 ounces spaghetti, cooked and drained
2 (10-ounce) packages frozen chopped spinach,
   thawed and squeezed dry
4 cups chopped cooked chicken
1 pound fresh mushrooms, sliced
3 tablespoons butter
1/4 cup green onions, sliced
5 tablespoons butter
1/2 cup all-purpose flour
1/4 cup chopped fresh parsley
2 1/2 teaspoons salt
1/2 teaspoon white pepper
2 cups milk
3 ounces Swiss cheese, shredded
2 tablespoons lemon juice
3/4 cup dry white wine
1/4 cup sherry
2 (8-ounce) cans artichoke hearts, drained and chopped

Sauté the garlic in 2 tablespoons butter until golden brown. Add to the spaghetti in a bowl and toss to combine. Pour into a well-greased 3-quart baking dish. Layer the spinach and chicken over the spaghetti. Sauté the mushrooms in 3 tablespoons butter in a skillet until tender. Remove from the skillet. Sauté the green onions in 5 tablespoons butter in the skillet for several minutes. Stir in the flour, parsley, salt and white pepper. Whisk in the milk. Cook until thickened, stirring constantly. Add the cheese and stir until melted. Add the lemon juice, wine, sherry, artichokes and mushrooms and stir well. Pour over the chicken. Bake at 350 degrees for 30 to 40 minutes or until bubbly.

Makes 6 to 8 servings

Note: This is a great dish for a luncheon or brunch. Even men like it.

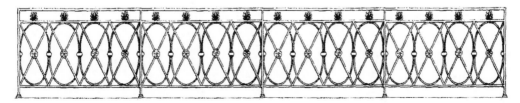

chicken Tetrazzini

6 ounces thin spaghetti, cooked and drained
12 ounces fresh mushrooms, sliced
1 small green bell pepper, slivered
1/4 cup (1/2 stick) butter or margarine
3 tablespoons all-purpose flour
2 teaspoons salt
1/4 teaspoon pepper
2 1/2 cups light cream
4 cups diced cooked chicken or turkey
2 pimentos, chopped
2 egg yolks, beaten
Grated Parmesan cheese

Divide the spaghetti among 6 individual broiler-proof baking dishes or spoon it into a large shallow baking dish. Sauté the mushrooms and bell pepper in the butter in a skillet for 5 minutes. Whisk in the flour, salt and pepper. Add the cream. Cook until thickened, stirring constantly. Stir in the chicken and pimentos. Cook until heated through. Stir a small amount of the sauce into the beaten egg yolks; stir the egg yolks into the sauce. Pour over the spaghetti. Sprinkle with cheese. Bake at 300 degrees for 45 minutes or until bubbly. Place under a hot broiler to brown slightly.

Makes 6 servings

"*Wine* makes a symphony of a good meal."
—*Fernande Garvin,* The Art of French Cooking

white Bean and chicken chili

4 skinless chicken breasts
1 onion, quartered
2 ribs celery
4 cups water
1 large onion, chopped
1 red bell pepper, chopped
1 jalapeño chile, seeded and
  chopped
1/4 cup vegetable oil
3 garlic cloves, minced
1/4 cup (1/2 stick) unsalted butter
1/4 cup all-purpose flour
1 tablespoon chili powder
1 tablespoon cumin

1/2 teaspoon Tabasco sauce,
  or to taste
1/4 teaspoon cayenne pepper
1/2 teaspoon salt, or to taste
1 teaspoon white pepper, or to taste
1 cup half-and-half
1 (14-ounce) can diced tomatoes
4 (15-ounce) cans Great Northern
  beans, drained and rinsed
1 (4-ounce) can whole mild green
  chiles, drained and chopped
1 cup (4 ounces) shredded
  Monterey Jack cheese

Combine the chicken breasts, quartered onion, celery and water in a saucepan. Bring to a boil. Reduce the heat and simmer for 30 to 40 minutes. Remove the chicken breasts and let stand until cool. Strain and reserve the stock. Chop the chicken into 1/2-inch pieces, discarding the bones.

Sauté the chopped onion, bell pepper and jalapeño chile in the oil in a large heavy-bottomed pan over moderate heat until tender. Add the garlic. Cook for 1 minute longer. Reduce the heat to low. Add the butter and heat until it foams. Whisk in the flour, chili powder, cumin, Tabasco sauce, cayenne pepper, salt and white pepper. Cook over low heat for 3 to 4 minutes or until the flour begins to turn golden brown, stirring constantly. Add 2 cups of the reserved stock gradually. Stir in the half-and-half. Simmer for 5 minutes or until slightly thickened, stirring constantly. Stir in the tomatoes, beans, green chiles and chopped chicken. Cook over low heat for 20 to 30 minutes. Stir in the cheese. Thin with additional chicken stock, if desired. Top each serving with a dollop of sour cream, chopped cilantro and a tablespoon of tomato salsa or tomatillo sauce.

Makes 6 servings

Note: Even picky children will love his dish. Pack it in a lunch box thermos to enjoy at school on a cold winter day.

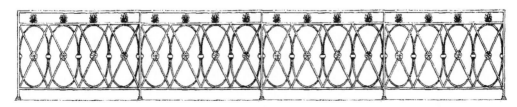

Salmon Teriyaki

2 cups soy sauce
1/2 (1-pound) package brown sugar
1/2 teaspoon dry mustard
1 garlic clove, minced
1/2 tablespoon minced fresh ginger
1/2 cup white wine
6 salmon fillets, or 1 (6- to 7-pound) side of salmon
3 tablespoons toasted sesame seeds (optional)

Combine the soy sauce, brown sugar, dry mustard, garlic, ginger and wine in a sealable plastic bag. And the salmon fillets and seal. Marinate in the refrigerator for 30 minutes. Remove the salmon and place on a grill tray lined with aluminum foil; discard the marinade. Grill, loosely covered with another piece of foil, over hot coals for 11 to 16 minutes or until the salmon flakes easily. Top with the sesame seeds.

Makes 6 servings

"There is one thing more exasperating than a wife who can cook and won't and that's a wife who can't cook and will."
—*Robert Frost* (1874–1963)

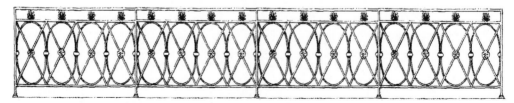

Mustard-Grilled Red Snapper

2/3 cup Dijon mustard
1¼ cups red wine vinegar
1¼ teaspoons ground red pepper
4 red snapper fillets
Sprigs of fresh parsley
Red peppercorns

Combine the Dijon mustard, vinegar and red pepper in a small bowl and mix well. Coat the fillets thoroughly with the mustard mixture. Grill, covered, over medium-hot coals for 8 minutes or until the fish flakes easily. Garnish with parsley and peppercorns.

Makes 4 to 6 servings

Snapper with Cilantro Sauce

3 cups loosely packed fresh cilantro
½ cup water
4 teaspoons fresh lime juice
4 fresh red or green Thai chiles, seeded and chopped
¼ teaspoon salt
Pinch of sugar
4 (4-ounce) red snapper, flounder, sole or orange roughy fillets

Combine the cilantro, water, lime juice, Thai chiles, salt and sugar in a blender and process until smooth. Place the fillets on 4 lightly oiled squares of foil. Spread 2 teaspoons of the cilantro sauce on each fillet. Fold the foil up around the fish and crimp the edges to seal. Place the packets on a baking sheet. Bake at 400 degrees for 10 minutes or until the fish flakes easily. Serve with the remaining sauce.

Makes 4 servings

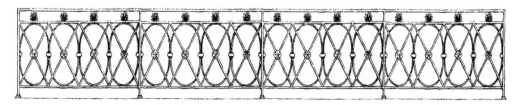

crab cakes

1 pound jumbo lump crab meat, shells removed
4 scallions, minced (green parts only)
1 tablespoon chopped fresh herbs, such as cilantro,
   dill weed, parsley or basil
1 1/2 teaspoons Old Bay seasoning
2 tablespoons to 1/4 cup fine dry bread crumbs
1/4 cup mayonnaise
Salt and white pepper to taste
1 egg, beaten
1/4 cup all-purpose flour
1/4 cup vegetable oil

Combine the crab meat, scallions, herbs, Old Bay seasoning, 2 tablespoons bread crumbs and the mayonnaise in a bowl and mix gently. Add the salt and pepper. Stir in the egg. Add additional bread crumbs if necessary until the mixture holds together. Divide into 4 portions. Shape each portion into a fat round cake 3 inches wide and 1 1/2 inches thick. Place on a baking sheet lined with waxed paper. Chill, covered with plastic wrap, for 30 minutes or up to 24 hours. Coat the crab cakes with the flour. Heat the oil in a large nonstick skillet over medium-high heat. Panfry the crab cakes in the oil for 4 to 5 minutes on each side or until crisp and brown.

Makes 4 servings

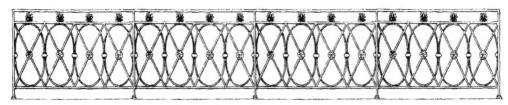

Easy Étouffée

1/2 cup (1 stick) butter
1 tablespoon all-purpose flour
1 onion, chopped
1/2 green bell pepper, chopped
2 or 3 ribs celery, chopped
2 garlic cloves, minced or pressed
1 (10-ounce) can cream of celery soup
1 pound crawfish tails with fat, or
   1 1/2 pounds medium shrimp, peeled
1/2 cup chopped green onions (green parts only)
1 teaspoon parsley
1 teaspoon salt
1 teaspoon black pepper
Cayenne pepper to taste
Paprika
Hot cooked rice

Melt the butter in a large saucepan and whisk in the flour. Add the onion, bell pepper, celery and garlic. Cook until the vegetables are tender, stirring occasionally. Stir in the soup. Simmer, covered, for 20 minutes. Add the crawfish, green onions, parsley, salt, black pepper and cayenne pepper. Cook over low heat for 5 minutes for the crawfish or just until the shrimp are pink. Add enough paprika to turn the sauce pink. Serve over rice.

Makes 6 servings

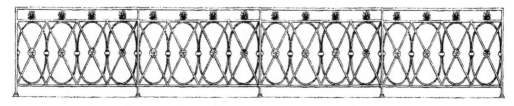

shrimp à la crème

1¹/₂ pounds shrimp, peeled and deveined
¹/₃ cup butter
8 ounces sliced fresh mushrooms
1¹/₂ cups sour cream
1 teaspoon soy sauce
1 tablespoon paprika
Salt and pepper to taste
Grated Parmesan cheese

Sauté the shrimp in the butter in a skillet for 3 minutes. Add the mushrooms. Cook for 8 minutes longer. Combine the sour cream, soy sauce, paprika, salt and pepper in a small saucepan and warm over low heat. Add to the shrimp mixture. Cook over low heat for 4 minutes or until thick and smooth, stirring constantly. Spoon into 4 buttered scallop shells or a buttered baking dish. Sprinkle with grated Parmesan cheese. Broil for 4 minutes or until the top is golden brown.

Makes 4 servings

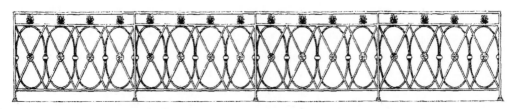

Low Country Shrimp Boil

1/3 pound (2/3 cup) butter
1/3 cup salt
1 bag shrimp boil
2 lemons, cut into halves
2 tablespoons Worcestershire sauce
1 teaspoon Tabasco sauce
New potatoes, quartered (2 to 3 per person)
Corn on the cob (1 to 2 half ears per person)
Kielbasa sausage, cut into 3/4-inch slices
  (4 ounces per person)
Medium unpeeled shrimp (8 ounces per person)

Fill a large stockpot half full of water. Add the butter, salt, shrimp boil, lemons, Worcestershire sauce and Tabasco sauce. Bring to a boil. Add the potatoes, corn, sausage and shrimp one at a time, waiting for the cooking liquid to return to a boil before adding the next ingredient. Cook the potatoes for 5 minutes, the corn for 4 minutes, the sausage for 4 minutes and the shrimp for 4 minutes or until they turn pink. Drain off the liquid. Serve the shrimp boil with cocktail sauce and crusty bread.

Serves 10

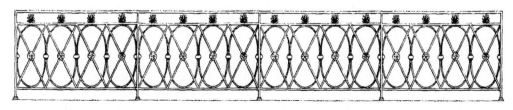

shrimp and scallops stroganoff

1 pound large shrimp, peeled and deveined
1 pound scallops
3 tablespoons butter or margarine
8 ounces fresh mushrooms, sliced
2 tablespoons dry sherry or medium sherry
2 tablespoons all-purpose flour, or 1 tablespoon cornstarch
1 envelope chicken bouillon
1 cup water
$1/8$ teaspoon pepper
1 cup sour cream
Hot cooked rice
2 teaspoons minced fresh parsley

Rinse the shrimp and scallops; pat dry. Sauté in 2 tablespoons of the butter in a 12-inch skillet over medium-high heat for 5 minutes or until the shrimp are pink and the scallops are tender. Removed with a slotted spoon to a bowl. Add the remaining tablespoon butter, mushrooms and sherry. Cook until the mushrooms are tender, stirring frequently. Whisk the flour, bouillon, water and pepper together in a bowl and stir into the mushrooms. Bring to a boil, stirring constantly. Reduce the heat to low and stir in the sour cream. Add the shrimp and scallops. Cook over low heat until heated through. Serve over rice. Garnish with the parsley.

Makes 6 to 8 servings

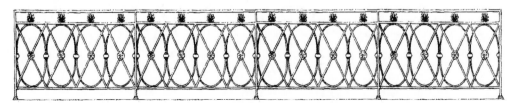

Four-Cheese Lasagna

The sauce:
2 ribs celery, chopped
1 small onion, chopped
1 garlic clove, minced
1/4 cup olive oil
1 (8-ounce) can tomato paste
1 tablespoon chopped fresh parsley
1/8 teaspoon basil
Salt and pepper to taste

The lasagna:
8 ounces ricotta cheese or cottage cheese
1/4 cup (1 ounce) grated Parmesan cheese
2 eggs
2 tablespoons chopped fresh parsley
6 lasagna noodles, cooked and drained
12 ounces medium-sharp Cheddar cheese, shredded
12 ounces mozzarella cheese, shredded

For the sauce, sauté the celery, onion and garlic in the olive oil in a skillet until barely tender. Stir in the tomato paste, parsley, basil, salt and pepper. Simmer for 30 to 45 minutes, stirring frequently.

For the lasagna, combine the ricotta cheese, Parmesan cheese, eggs and parsley in a bowl and mix well. Layer 1/2 of the sauce, 3 of the noodles, 1/2 of the Cheddar cheese and 1/2 of the mozzarella cheese in a greased 8×12-inch baking dish. Spoon the ricotta mixture over the top. Layer the remaining sauce, noodles, Cheddar cheese and mozzarella cheese over the ricotta mixture. Bake, covered with foil, at 350 degrees for 30 minutes. Remove the foil. Bake for 30 minutes longer.

Makes 8 servings

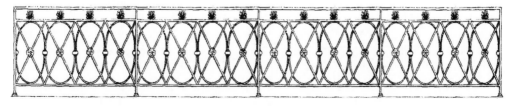

chiles Rellenos

4 canned whole green chiles, drained
1 pound sharp Cheddar cheese, shredded
1 pound Monterey Jack cheese, shredded
2 egg whites
1 (8-ounce) can tomato sauce
1 (5-ounce) can evaporated milk
2 egg yolks, beaten
3 tablespoons all-purpose flour
Salt and pepper to taste

Flatten the green chiles; pat dry. Place in the bottom of a greased 9×13-inch baking dish. Sprinkle the Cheddar cheese and Monterey Jack cheese over the chiles. Beat the egg whites in a bowl until stiff peaks form. Combine the tomato sauce, evaporated milk, egg yolks, flour, salt and pepper in a bowl and mix well. Fold into the beaten egg whites. Pour over the cheese. Bake at 325 degrees for 45 minutes or until light brown. Let stand for 10 minutes before serving. Cut into squares.

Makes 10 to 12 servings

Note: This is also a great side dish for any Mexican meal. It's easy and delicious.

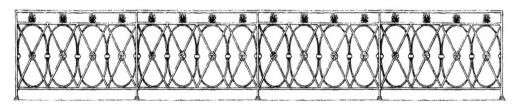

vegetables & side Dishes

"when one has tasted watermelon,
he knows what the angels eat."
Mark Twain

carrot and cauliflower Medley

1 pound carrots, cut into 1/4-inch diagonal pieces
1 head cauliflower, broken into florets
2 tablespoons butter
2 tablespoons all-purpose flour
1 tablespoon Dijon mustard
1/2 teaspoon salt
1 cup chicken broth
1/2 cup heavy cream or whipping cream
1 1/2 cups (6 ounces) shredded Swiss cheese
2 green onions, sliced (include green tops)

Cook the carrots and cauliflower in boiling salted water to cover for 7 to 10 minutes or until tender-crisp; drain. Plunge the vegetables into cold water; drain again. Melt the butter in a saucepan over medium heat. Stir in the flour, Dijon mustard and salt. Add the broth and cream gradually. Cook until thickened, stirring constantly. Add 1 cup of the cheese and stir until melted. Combine the vegetables and sauce in a 2-quart baking dish. Sprinkle with the remaining cheese. Bake at 350 degrees for 15 minutes. Garnish with the green onions.

Makes 6 to 8 servings

Note: This is a good vegetable dish to prepare ahead of time. Assemble the casserole and chill, covered, until baking time.

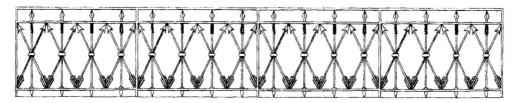

carrot soufflé

2 cups puréed cooked carrots
2 teaspoons lemon juice
1 cup milk
1/2 cup (1 stick) butter, softened
2 tablespoons minced or grated onion
3 eggs, beaten
1/4 cup sugar
1 tablespoon all-purpose flour
1 teaspoon salt
1/4 teaspoon ground cinnamon

Combine the carrots, lemon juice, milk, butter, onion, eggs, sugar, flour, salt and cinnamon in a bowl and beat until smooth. Pour into a lightly buttered 2-quart soufflé dish. Bake, uncovered, at 350 degrees for 45 to 60 minutes or until the center is firm to the touch.

Makes 6 to 8 servings

Note: The carrots may be cooked and puréed hours ahead of time. Mix in the lemon juice and cover tightly until ready to mix with the other ingredients. This is a different, delicious, and never-fail recipe. The sweetness of the soufflé will dictate the choice of menu. It is lovely with Roast Veal Dijon (page 92) and fresh young asparagus.

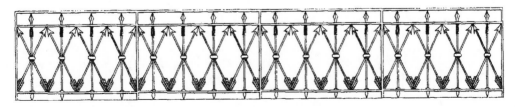

Spicy Eggplant

2 eggs, beaten
$1/2$ cup cornstarch
1 eggplant, peeled and cut into large slices
Vegetable oil for frying
1 garlic clove, minced
2 tablespoons vegetable oil
2 cups water
2 tablespoons cornstarch
3 tablespoons soy sauce
3 tablespoons white vinegar
$1/2$ cup sugar
1 carrot, julienned
1 cup bean sprouts
1 cup diced green onions
3 or 4 chile peppers, diced

Combine the eggs, $1/2$ cup cornstarch and a splash of water in a shallow bowl and mix well. Dip the eggplant in the egg mixture. Fry in hot oil until brown; drain on paper towels. Sauté the garlic in 2 tablespoons oil in a saucepan until golden brown. Combine the water and 2 tablespons cornstarch in a bowl. Stir in the cornstarch mixture, soy sauce, vinegar and sugar. Bring to a boil. Add the carrot, bean sprouts, green onions and chile peppers. Simmer until the vegetables are tender. Add the eggplant. Cook until heated through.

Makes 4 to 6 servings

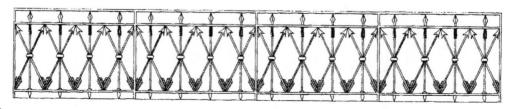

Hot Marinated Green Beans

2 (16-ounce) cans French-style green beans, drained and rinsed
2 large onions, sliced and separated into rings
1 pound bacon
1/2 cup vinegar
1/2 cup packed light brown sugar

Layer the green beans and onion rings half at a time in a 2-quart baking dish. Cook the bacon in a skillet until crisp; drain, reserving 1/2 cup of the drippings. Crumble the bacon over the layers. Combine the reserved drippings, vinegar and brown sugar in a bowl and mix well. Pour over the green beans. Marinate, covered, in the refrigerator for 8 to 10 hours. Bake at 350 degrees for 45 minutes.

Makes 6 servings

Lemon Pepper Green Beans

1 pound green beans, rinsed and trimmed
1/4 cup almonds, sliced
2 tablespoons butter
2 teaspoons lemon pepper

Place the green beans in a vegetable steamer over 1 inch of hot water. Cook, covered, for 10 minutes or until tender-crisp. Sauté the almonds in the butter in a skillet over medium heat until light brown. Season with the lemon pepper. Stir in the green beans and toss to combine.

Makes 4 to 6 servings

Note: These beans are a bit tangy, spicy, and crunchy.

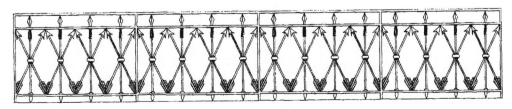

Potato and Fennel Gratin

1 tablespoon olive oil
1 large red onion, thinly sliced
1/2 teaspoon salt
Freshly ground pepper to taste
1 cup heavy cream or whipping cream
2 ounces Roquefort cheese, crumbled
2 egg yolks
1 teaspoon salt
4 russet potatoes, peeled and cut into 1/16-inch slices
1 fennel bulb, trimmed and cut into 1/16-inch slices

Heat the olive oil in a sauté pan over medium heat. Add the onion, 1/2 teaspoon salt and pepper. Sauté for 7 to 8 minutes or until the onion begins to brown. Combine the cream, 1/2 of the cheese, the egg yolks, 1 teaspoon salt and pepper in a small saucepan. Cook over medium-low heat for 3 to 5 minutes or until the cheese melts and the sauce begins to steam. Layer the potatoes, onion and fennel 1/3 at a time in a 9-inch baking dish. Pour the cream sauce over the vegetables. Top with the remaining cheese. Bake, covered with foil, at 350 degrees for 30 minutes. Increase the heat to 450 degrees. Bake, uncovered, for 15 to 18 minutes longer or until brown and bubbly. Let stand for 10 minutes before serving.

Makes 4 to 6 servings

Note: Try this delicious gratin with pork roast or baked chicken and a crisp green salad with a simple vinaigrette.

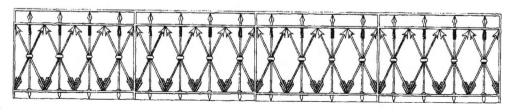

Parmesan Potatoes

2 or 3 Irish potatoes, or 6 to 8 new potatoes, thinly sliced
1/4 to 1/2 cup (1/2 to 1 stick) butter, melted
Minced garlic or garlic powder (optional)
Salt and pepper to taste
Grated Parmesan cheese

Arrange the potato slices in a single layer on a baking sheet. Combine the butter and garlic in a small bowl. Brush the potatoes with the butter. Sprinkle with salt, pepper and cheese. Bake at 350 degrees for 30 to 40 minutes.

Makes 3 to 4 servings

Potato Casserole

1 cup milk
1 cup (4 ounces) shredded Cheddar cheese
2 teaspoons chopped green onion tops
1/2 teaspoon salt
4 potatoes, peeled, cooked and mashed
5 slices bacon, crisp-cooked and crumbled
1 cup (4 ounces) shredded Cheddar cheese

Scald the milk in a small saucepan. Add 1 cup cheese, the green onions and salt and stir until the cheese is melted. Combine the cheese sauce, potatoes and bacon in a large bowl and mix well. Spoon into a greased 1-quart baking dish. Sprinkle with 1 cup cheese. Bake at 350 degrees for 10 minutes or until the cheese is melted.

Makes 4 to 6 servings

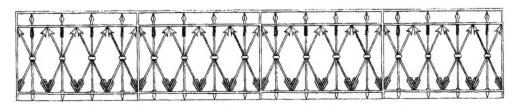

Cheesy Scalloped Potatoes

1/3 cup chopped green onions
1/3 cup chopped red bell pepper
1 garlic clove, minced
1/4 teaspoon ground red pepper
3 tablespoons butter
2 cups heavy cream or whipping cream
3/4 cup milk
3/4 teaspoon salt
1/4 teaspoon black pepper
21/2 pounds red potatoes, thinly sliced, or
   2 packages sliced fresh potatoes
1 cup (4 ounces) shredded Swiss cheese
1/4 cup (1 ounce) grated Parmesan cheese

Sauté the green onions, bell pepper, garlic and red pepper in the butter in a skillet for 2 to 3 minutes, stirring constantly. Stir in the cream, milk, salt and black pepper. Add the potatoes. Simmer for 15 minutes or until the potatoes begin to soften. Stir in the Swiss cheese. Pour into a 9×13-inch baking dish. Top with the Parmesan cheese. Bake, uncovered, at 350 degrees for 45 minutes.

Makes 6 servings

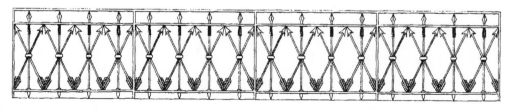

spinach casserole

8 ounces cream cheese, softened
$^1/_2$ cup (1 stick) butter, softened
1 (10-ounce) package frozen spinach
2 tablespoons lemon juice
Bread crumbs

Combine the cream cheese and butter in a bowl and mix well. Cook the spinach in a saucepan of boiling water just until thawed; drain well. Stir into the cream cheese mixture. Add the lemon juice and mix well. Spoon into a baking dish. Sprinkle with bread crumbs. Bake at 350 degrees for 25 to 30 minutes or until heated through and the top is brown.

Makes 4 to 6 servings

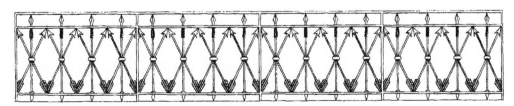

Frito Squash Bake

2 pounds yellow squash, sliced, or 3
 packages frozen squash, thawed
1 onion, diced
2 tablespoons brown sugar
1 (10-ounce) can cream of
 mushroom soup

2 tablespoons butter
1 teaspoon salt
1 small package corn chips,
 lightly crushed
1 cup (4 ounces) shredded
 Cheddar cheese

Cook the squash, onion and brown sugar in a saucepan over medium-low
heat until the squash is tender. Stir in the soup, butter and salt. Layer 1/2 of
the squash, all of the Fritos, the remaining squash and cheese in a 9×13-inch
baking dish. Bake at 400 degrees for 25 minutes.

Makes 10 to 12 servings

Aunt Fanny's Baked Squash

3 pounds summer squash, sliced
1/2 cup chopped onion
2 eggs, beaten
1/4 cup (1/2 stick) butter, melted
1 tablespoon sugar

1 teaspoon salt
1/2 teaspoon pepper
1/2 cup crushed butter crackers
1/4 cup (1/2 stick) butter, melted

Cook the squash in boiling water to cover in a saucepan until tender; drain
and mash. Combine the squash, onion, eggs, 1/4 cup butter, the sugar, salt
and pepper in a bowl and mix well. Spoon into a baking dish. Combine the
cracker crumbs and 1/4 cup butter in a small bowl and mix well. Sprinkle over
the squash mixture. Bake at 375 degrees for 1 hour or until brown on top.

Makes 6 to 8 servings

Note: This recipe is from the famous Aunt Fanny's Cabin Restaurant in
Atlanta, Georgia.

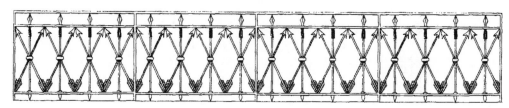

Tomato Chutney

1 pound Granny Smith apples, peeled and quartered
3 green bell peppers, quartered
6 shallots, coarsely chopped
3/4 cup raisins
3 pounds tomatoes, peeled and coarsely chopped
3 cups malt vinegar
2 cups packed light brown sugar
2 tablespoons mustard seeds
1 tablespoon finely chopped fresh mint
1/4 cup salt

Combine the apples, bell peppers, shallots and raisins in a food processor and pulse several times. Remove to a heavy saucepan. Stir in the tomatoes, vinegar, brown sugar, mustard seeds, mint and salt. Boil for 10 minutes, stirring occasionally. Reduce the heat and simmer for 15 minutes or until thickened. Store, tightly covered, in the refrigerator for up to 3 weeks.

Makes about 4 cups

'It's difficult to think anything but pleasant thoughts
while eating a homegrown tomato."
—Louis Grizzard

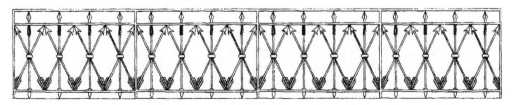

Fresh Tomato Tart

3 to 4 pie pastry sheets
8 large vine-ripened tomatoes, seeded and sliced
1/4 cup balsamic vinegar
1/4 cup olive oil
2 tablespoons chopped fresh thyme or basil
2 tablespoons chopped fresh parsley
Freshly grated or shaved Parmesan cheese
8 ounces shredded mozzarella cheese
2 cups mixed salad greens or arugula
Salt and pepper to taste

Cut eight 5-inch rounds from the pastry sheets. Place on a baking sheet. Chill for 30 minutes. Bake at 400 degrees for 10 minutes. Cover with another baking tray. Bake for 8 minutes longer or just until golden brown. Remove the rounds to a wire rack to cool. Arrange the tomato slices in a circular pattern on the pastry rounds, covering the entire pastry. Brush with half of the vinegar and olive oil. Sprinkle with the thyme, parsley, Parmesan cheese and mozzarella cheese. Broil the tarts on the top oven rack or bake at 500 degrees until the cheese is melted and just turning golden brown around the edges, watching carefully to prevent burning. Toss the salad greens with the remaining vinegar and olive oil. Season with salt and pepper. Arrange 1/4 cup greens on each tomato tart. Top with a sprinkle of Parmesan cheese.

Makes 8 servings

"Polenta? Oh you mean Italian grits."
—*Unknown*

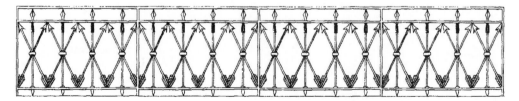

Macaroni Casserole

8 ounces macaroni, cooked and drained
1 (10-ounce) can cream of mushroom soup
1 pound shredded cheese
1 onion, chopped
1 green bell pepper, chopped
1 (2-ounce) jar diced pimento
1 cup mayonnaise
1/4 cup (1/2 stick) butter, melted
Crushed butter crackers

Combine the macaroni, soup, cheese, onion, bell pepper, pimento and mayonnaise in a bowl and mix well. Pour into a greased baking dish. Combine the butter with enough crushed crackers to make a crumbly topping. Sprinkle over the macaroni mixture. Bake at 400 degrees for 30 to 40 minutes or until golden brown on top.

Makes 6 to 8 servings

Penne Pasta

1 pound penne
1 cup (4 ounces) goat cheese, crumbled
3 tablespoons olive oil
1/4 cup chopped fresh basil
1/4 cup chopped fresh parsley
3 tablespoons chopped fresh mint
3 tablespoons chopped fresh chives
1/2 teaspoon minced garlic
1/8 to 1/4 teaspoon (or more) red pepper flakes

Cook the penne using the package directions; drain, reserving 1/2 cup of the cooking liquid. Combine the goat cheese, olive oil, basil, parsley, mint, chives, garlic and red pepper flakes in a bowl. Stir in the reserved cooking liquid and mix well. Stir in the penne. Serve immediately.

Makes 6 to 8 servings

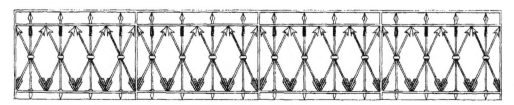

Pasta and Peppers Gratín

8 ounces mostaccioli or rigatoni
2 tablespoons olive oil
2 large red bell peppers
2 large yellow bell peppers
1 garlic clove, crushed
1/4 cup olive oil
1 (2-ounce) can anchovies, drained and chopped
1 can black olives, drained and 1/2 of the olives chopped
1 tablespoon capers
Salt and pepper to taste
2 tablespoons bread crumbs
2 tablespoons grated Parmesan cheese
2 tablespoons olive oil

Cook the pasta in boiling water in a large pot until just done; drain and return to the pot. Add 2 tablespoons olive oil and toss to combine. Broil the red and yellow bell peppers until the skins are blistered and blackened, turning frequently. Cool in a paper bag. Cut into strips, discarding the seeds and skins. Sauté the bell peppers and garlic briefly in 1/4 cup olive oil in a 10-inch skillet. Stir in the anchovies, chopped olives, capers, salt and pepper. Combine the bread crumbs and cheese in a small bowl and mix well. Layer 1/2 of the crumb mixture and 1/2 of the bell pepper mixture in a 2-quart oblong baking dish. Cover with the pasta. Layer the remaining bell pepper mixture and crumb mixture over the pasta. Drizzle 2 tablespoons olive oil over the top. Bake at 375 degrees for 20 minutes. Garnish with the whole olives and additional Parmesan cheese.

Makes 4 to 6 servings

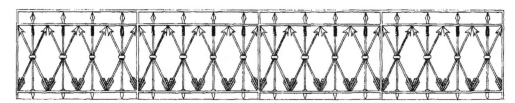

Corn Bread Dressing

1 large onion, chopped
1 cup chopped celery and
  celery leaves
1/2 cup (1 stick) butter
1 large skillet day-old southern
  corn bread, crumbled
3 slices day-old white
  bread, crumbled

3 eggs, beaten
1 1/2 to 2 teaspoons sage
1 teaspoon salt
1/2 teaspoon pepper
5 cups chicken broth (preferably
  from a 2- to 3-pound cooked
  chicken)

Cook the onion and celery in the butter in a skillet until tender. Combine with the corn bread, white bread, eggs, sage, salt and pepper in a large bowl and mix well. Add enough of the broth to make a very moist dressing. Spoon into a lightly greased baking dish. Bake at 400 degrees for 45 minutes or until brown.

Makes 6 to 8 servings

Newer Super Grits

1 quart milk (whole or 2 percent)
1 cup grits (not instant)
6 small slices Gruyère cheese
1/2 cup (1 stick) margarine

1/3 cup milk
1/3 cup butter
1/3 cup grated Parmesan cheese

Combine 1 quart milk, the grits, Gruyère cheese and margarine in a saucepan. Bring to a boil. Reduce the heat and simmer for 20 minutes or until done, stirring frequently. Stir in 1/3 cup milk and the butter. Pour into a greased baking dish. Top with the Parmesan cheese. Bake at 350 degrees for 20 minutes or until bubbly.

Makes 6 servings

Note: This grits casserole has no eggs whatsoever. It's a hit every time!

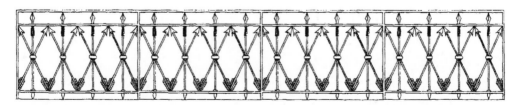

Grits, Turnip Greens and Ham Casserole

1 pound turnip greens, washed, chopped and
  stems removed, or 1 package frozen chopped turnip greens
8 ounces country ham, finely chopped (prosciutto works best)
1 large onion, chopped
4 garlic cloves, chopped
6 tablespoons butter
1 cup quick-cooking grits or coarsely ground regular grits
3 cups milk
1 cup heavy cream or whipping cream
2 cups (8 ounces) grated Parmesan cheese
2 tablespoons chopped fresh parsley
1/2 teaspoon thyme
1/2 cup dry white wine
2 eggs, beaten
Salt and pepper to taste.
Grated Parmesan cheese

Wilt the fresh turnip greens in boiling water in a large saucepan or thaw
the frozen ones; drain well. Sauté the ham, onion and garlic in the butter in
a skillet until the onion is tender. Cook the grits in the milk and cream in a
saucepan until thickened. Stir in 2 cups cheese, the parsley and thyme. Let
cool. Combine the turnip greens, ham mixture and grits in a large bowl and
mix well. Stir in the wine, eggs, salt and pepper. Pour into a greased baking
dish. Sprinkle with additional cheese. Bake at 400 degrees for 20 minutes.

Makes 6 servings

Note: This casserole will accompany any hearty meat well.

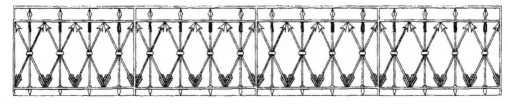

Polenta

12 cups water
1 tablespoon salt
2 large garlic cloves
3 cups polenta (white grits)
12 ounces sharp white Cheddar cheese, shredded
8 ounces mascarpone cheese
3 tablespoons butter, melted
$1/4$ teaspoon white pepper
1 tablespoon butter

Bring the water, salt and garlic to a boil in a large heavy saucepan or Dutch oven over high heat. Add the polenta gradually, whisking until smooth. Reduce the heat to medium-low. Cook for 12 minutes. Remove from the heat. Add $1/2$ of the Cheddar cheese, all of the mascarpone cheese, 3 tablespoons butter and the pepper and mix well. Pour into a buttered 10×15-inch glass baking dish. Top with the remaining Cheddar cheese. Dot with 1 tablespoon butter. Bake at 400 degrees for 30 minutes or until golden brown.

Makes 24 servings

Note: Polenta is good served with quail, dove, or a standing rib roast. You'll need to half the recipe unless you are feeding a crowd.

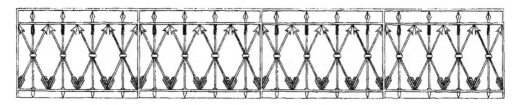

Savory Rice

1 1/2 cups long grain rice
2 1/2 cups chicken broth
3 ribs celery, coarsely chopped
1 bunch green onions, coarsely chopped
1 or 2 bay leaves
1/2 cup (1 stick) butter
2 garlic cloves, cut into halves
1 teaspoon salt

Cook the rice in the broth in a saucepan for 20 to 25 minutes or until tender. Let stand, covered, for 4 to 5 minutes. Fluff with a fork. Sauté the celery, green onions and bay leaves in the butter in a skillet until the celery is tender. Add the garlic and salt. Sauté a few minutes longer; remove and discard the garlic and bay leaves. Add the vegetables to the rice and stir gently.

Makes 4 to 6 servings

Note: This rice is especially good with chicken. The recipe doubles well.

Rice and Noodle Casserole

8 ounces thin noodles
1 cup (2 sticks) margarine
2 cups uncooked instant rice
2 cans chicken broth
2 cans French onion soup
1 can sliced mushrooms
1 package slivered almonds

Brown the noodles in the margarine in a skillet. Combine the noodles, rice, broth, soup, mushrooms and almonds in a large bowl and mix well. Pour into a greased 3-quart baking dish. Bake, uncovered, at 350 degrees for 45 minutes.

Makes 12 servings

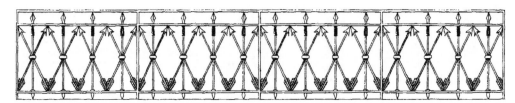

Sweets & Desserts

*"A gourmet who thinks of calories
is like a tart who looks at her watch."*

James Beard

Banana Flambé

1/4 cup (1/2 stick) butter or margarine
1 cup packed brown sugar
2 tablespoons water
4 ripe bananas, sliced lengthwise and halved
1 cup ground walnuts
1/2 cup flaked coconut
2 tablespoons Puerto Rican or Bacardi dark rum
Cherry preserves

Melt the butter with the brown sugar in a skillet, stirring constantly until liquified. Add the water and stir until smooth. Place the bananas flat side down in the butter mixture. Cook for 2 minutes on each side. Remove from the heat. Sprinkle the walnuts evenly over the bananas and let stand for 1 minute. Sprinkle the coconut over the walnuts. Simmer for 3 minutes. Remove from the heat. Drizzle the rum over the bananas. Light with a long match or lighter. Shake the skillet gently until the flames die down. Spoon into individual dishes. Top each serving with cherry preserves. Serve with ice cream or whipped topping, if desired.

Makes 8 servings

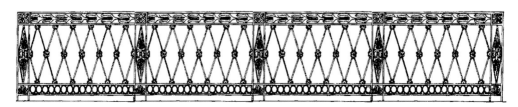

Blueberry Torte

1 cup sugar
1/2 cup (1 stick) butter, softened
1 cup all-purpose flour, sifted
1 teaspoon baking powder
2 eggs
Salt to taste
1 pint (or more) fresh blueberries
Sugar
Ground cinnamon
Lemon juice
All-purpose flour

Cream 1 cup sugar and the butter in a bowl until light and fluffy. Add 1 cup flour, the baking powder, eggs and salt. Beat until smooth. Spoon into a buttered 9-inch springform pan. Cover the entire surface with the blueberries. Sprinkle with sugar, cinnamon, lemon juice and a little flour. Bake at 350 degrees for 1 hour. Serve warm with vanilla ice cream or whipped cream.

Makes 8 servings

Note: You may substitute sliced apples, pitted Italian plums (24 halves placed skin side up) or sliced peaches for the blueberries. Frozen or canned blueberries or peaches may also be used, but be sure to rinse and drain the fruit well if using canned.

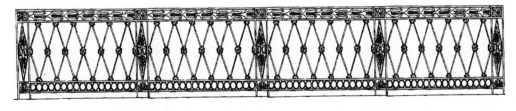

Cherry Betty

1 can cherry pie filling
1/3 teaspoon almond extract
1/2 cup packed brown sugar
3/4 teaspoon ground cinnamon
1/4 teaspoon nutmeg
1/4 cup (1/2 stick) butter or margarine
2 cups cornflakes, lightly crushed

Combine the cherry pie filling and almond extract in a bowl and mix well. Pour into a shallow 1- to 1 1/2-quart baking dish. Combine the brown sugar, cinnamon and nutmeg in a bowl and mix well. Cut in the butter until crumbly. Stir in the cornflakes. Sprinkle evenly over the pie filling. Bake at 375 degrees for 20 minutes. Serve with vanilla ice cream.

Makes 6 to 8 servings

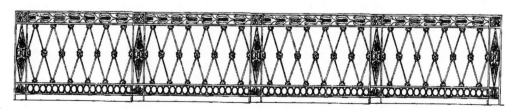

cherry cobbler

2 cans cherry pie filling
1 teaspoon almond extract (optional)
Cinnamon-sugar
1 small package yellow cake mix, or
   1/2 regular-size package yellow cake mix
1/2 to 1 cup chopped pecans
1/4 cup (1/2 stick) butter or margarine, melted

Combine the cherry pie filling and almond extract in a bowl and mix well. Pour into a 3-quart glass baking dish. Sprinkle with cinnamon-sugar. Layer the dry cake mix and pecans over the cherry filling. Drizzle with the butter. Bake at 350 degrees for 45 minutes or until light brown. Serve with whipped cream, whipped topping or ice cream.

Makes 8 to 10 servings

Note: This works just as well with apple pie filling or blueberry pie filling.

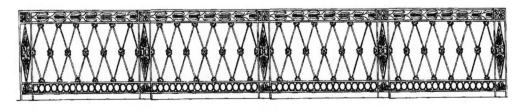

Goo

1 cup heavy cream or whipping cream
2 tablespoons confectioners' sugar
1/4 teaspoon vanilla extract
3/4 cup crushed pineapple in heavy syrup
1/2 cup chopped pecans
8 ounces miniature marshmallows
1/4 cup maraschino cherries (optional)

Whip the cream with the confectioners' sugar and vanilla in a mixing bowl until firm peaks form. Fold in the pineapple, pecans, marshmallows and cherries. Chill for 30 to 60 minutes. (Do not chill longer or the dessert will not be fluffy.) Spoon into parfait glasses or martini glasses. Serve with lady fingers or homemade pecan wedding cookies.

Makes 6 servings

"I prefer to regard dessert as I would imagine the perfect woman: subtle, a little bittersweet, not blowsy and extrovert. Delicately made up, not highly rouged. Holding back, not exposing everything and, of course, with a flavor that lasts."
—*Graham Kerr,* The Galloping Gourmet (1960s)

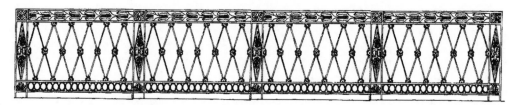

Lemon Crepes

The filling:
16 ounces cream cheese, softened
2/3 cup sugar
Juice of 1 lemon
1 tablespoon grated lemon zest
1 tablespoon light rum

The sauce:
1 cup (2 sticks) unsalted butter
1/4 cup sugar
Juice of 3 lemons (about 1/2 cup)
1 tablespoon grated lemon zest

The crepes:
2 eggs
1 cup milk
1/2 cup (1 stick) butter, melted
1 teaspoon vanilla extract
1/4 cup water
1/2 teaspoon salt
1 1/4 cups all-purpose flour
Vegetable oil

For the filling, beat the cream cheese in a mixing bowl until fluffy. Beat in the sugar gradually. Add the lemon juice, lemon zest and rum and beat until smooth.

For the sauce, melt the butter in a small saucepan over low heat. Add the sugar and stir until dissolved. Stir in the lemon juice and lemon zest.

For the crepes, combine the eggs, milk, butter, vanilla, water, salt and flour in a blender and process until smooth, scraping down the side several times. Add more water if necessary to form a batter that is just thick enough to coat a spoon. Lightly grease a small skillet or crepe pan with a paper towel dipped in oil. Heat the skillet until very hot. Pour enough of the batter into the skillet to thinly coat the bottom. Cook for 1 minute or until bubbles appear on the surface and the edge is golden brown. Turn the crepe. Cook for about 30 seconds. Remove to a paper towel. Repeat the process, using all of the remaining batter.

To assemble the crepes, spread a little of the filling down the center of each crepe. Roll up to enclose the filling. Spoon a little of the lemon sauce over the top.

Makes 9 or 10 (2-crepe) servings

Note: This recipe is from *The Commander's Palace New Orleans Cookbook.*

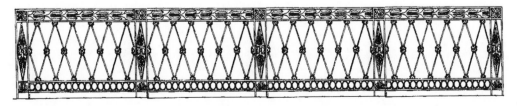

Stuffed Pears Milanese

4 ounces almonds, toasted and finely ground
4 maraschino cherries, finely chopped
3/4 cup confectioners' sugar
1/4 teaspoon almond extract
6 large firm pears, cut in half lengthwise and cored
1/2 cup dry sherry

Combine the almonds, cherries, confectioners' sugar and almond extract in a bowl and mix well. Spoon into the cored pear halves. Place in a baking dish. Pour the sherry over the pears. Bake at 350 degrees for 15 minutes or until the pears are just done. Serve hot or cold.

Makes 6 servings

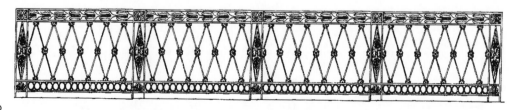

Strawberries with Peppermint whipped Topping

2 quarts large strawberries, washed and
  dried on paper towels
16 ounces whipped topping
2 sticks peppermint candy, crushed

Arrange the strawberries around the edge of a serving dish. Mound the whipped topping in the center. Sprinkle with the peppermint candy.

Makes 15 to 20 servings

Note: Peppermint candy gives whipped topping a holiday flavor and makes it a fun dip for strawberries. Add this dish to your brunch buffet table.

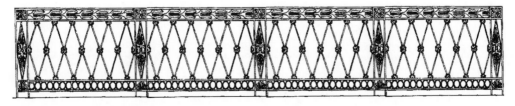

Ice Cream Sandwich Dessert

19 ice cream sandwiches
12 ounces whipped topping
1 cup salted peanuts
1 (11-ounce) jar hot fudge topping,
  warmed in the microwave

Layer the ice cream sandwiches, whipped topping and peanuts half at a time in a 9×13-inch baking dish. Spread the fudge topping over the top. Freeze, covered, for up to 2 months. Cut into squares.

Makes 10 to 12 servings

"The fricassee with dumplings is made by a Mrs. Miller whose husband has left her four times on account of her disposition and returned four times on account of her cooking and is still there."
—*Rex Stout,* Nero Wolfe

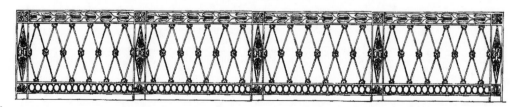

Buttermilk Sorbet

1 cup sugar
1 cup water
3 cups buttermilk
1 tablespoon fresh lemon juice

Combine the sugar and water in a saucepan over medium heat. Stir until the sugar is dissolved. Increase the heat to medium-high. Boil for 1 minute. Remove from the heat and let cool completely. Stir in the buttermilk and lemon juice. Pour into an ice cream freezer container. Freeze using the manufacturer's directions.

Makes 6 servings

"The washing of dishes does seem to me the most absurd and unsatisfactory business that I ever undertook. If, when once washed, they would remain clean forever and ever (which they ought in all reason to do, considering how much trouble it is,) there would be less occasion to grumble; but no sooner is it done, than it requires to be done again. On the whole, I have come to the resolution not to use more than one dish at each meal."
—*Nathaniel Hawthorne* (1844) while Mrs. Hawthorne was away

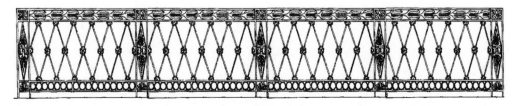

145

Glazed Fresh Apple Cake

The apple cake:
2 cups sugar
1 1/2 cups vegetable oil
2 eggs
3 cups all-purpose flour
1 teaspoon baking soda
1 teaspoon salt
3 cups diced peeled tart apples
1 cup chopped pecans or walnuts
2 teaspoons vanilla extract
1 teaspoon nutmeg
1 teaspoon ground cinnamon

The glaze:
1 cup packed brown sugar
1/2 cup (1 stick) butter
1/4 cup evaporated milk
1 teaspoon vanilla extract

For the cake, combine the sugar, oil and eggs in a large mixing bowl and beat well by hand. Combine the flour, baking soda and salt. Add to the sugar mixture and mix well. Stir in the apples, pecans, vanilla, nutmeg and cinnamon. (The batter will be stiff.) Spoon into a greased and floured tube or bundt pan. Bake at 350 degrees for 1 hour and 15 minutes or until firm to the touch. Cool in the pan for 10 minutes. Invert onto a serving plate.

For the glaze, combine the brown sugar, butter, evaporated milk and vanilla in a heavy saucepan. Bring to a boil. Cook for 5 minutes, stirring constantly. Remove from the heat. Beat for 1 minute with a spoon. Drizzle 1/2 of the glaze over the warm cake.

Makes 15 to 18 servings

Note: Use the leftover glaze as a dip for apples.

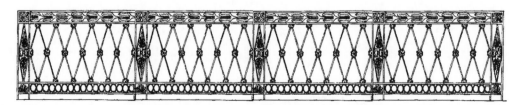

chocolate chip cake

4 eggs, beaten
1/2 cup sugar
3/4 cup vegetable oil
2/3 cup water
1 package yellow cake mix (not butter-flavored)
1 (6-ounce) package instant chocolate pudding mix
1 cup sour cream
1 cup (6 ounces) miniature semisweet chocolate chips

Combine the eggs, sugar, oil and water in a mixing bowl and mix well. Stir in the cake mix, pudding mix, sour cream and chocolate chips. Pour into a greased and floured bundt pan. Bake at 350 degrees for 1 hour or until the cake tests done.

Makes 16 servings

"When baking, follow directions. When cooking,
go by your own taste."
—*Laiko Bahrs*

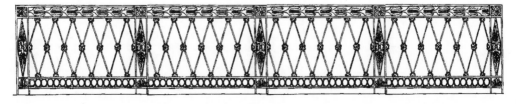

Mississippi Mud Cake

The cake:
4 eggs
2 cups sugar
1 cup (2 sticks) butter, melted
1 1/2 cups all-purpose flour
1/3 cup baking cocoa
1 teaspoon vanilla extract
1/2 cup chopped pecans (optional)
7 ounces marshmallow creme

The frosting:
1/2 cup (1 stick) butter
1/2 cup baking cocoa
1 (1-pound) package confectioners' sugar
6 tablespoons milk
1 teaspoon vanilla extract

For the cake, beat the eggs and sugar in a large mixing bowl. Combine the butter, flour, cocoa, vanilla and pecans in another bowl and mix well. Add to the egg mixture and mix well. Pour into a greased 9×13-inch cake pan. Bake at 350 degrees for 30 minutes. Spread the marshmallow creme over the hot cake. Let cool completely.

For the frosting, melt the butter in a small saucepan. Stir in the baking cocoa. Add the confectioners' sugar, milk and vanilla. Beat until smooth. Spread over the cooled cake.

Makes 12 servings

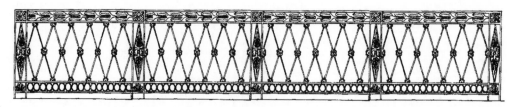

Secret cake

The cake:
2 cups sifted all-purpose flour
2 cups sugar
1/2 cup (1 stick) margarine
1/4 cup shortening
1 cup water
3 1/2 tablespoons baking cocoa
1/2 cup buttermilk
2 eggs, beaten
1 teaspoon vanilla extract
1 teaspoon baking soda
Pinch of salt

The frosting:
1/2 cup (1 stick) margarine
1/3 cup buttermilk
3 1/2 tablespoons baking cocoa
1 (1-pound) package confectioners' sugar
1 cup chopped nuts (optional)

For the cake, combine the flour and sugar in a large mixing bowl. Combine the margarine, shortening, water and cocoa in a saucepan. Bring to a boil, stirring constantly. Pour over the flour mixture and beat until smooth. Add the buttermilk, eggs, vanilla, baking soda and salt and mix well. Pour into a greased and floured 11×16-inch cake pan. (A broiler pan may be used.) Bake at 400 degrees for 20 minutes or until the cake tests done, being careful not to overbake.

For the frosting, combine the margarine, buttermilk and baking cocoa in a saucepan. Bring to a boil, stirring constantly until smooth. Remove from the heat. Beat in the confectioners' sugar and nuts. Frost the cake while it is still hot.

Makes 12 servings

Note: This cake is best made a day before serving. It freezes well, too.

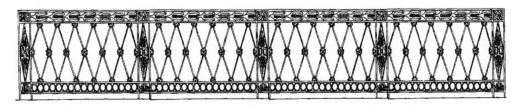

Coconut Lemonade Cake

The cake:
2 cups all-purpose flour
2 cups sugar
3 teaspoons baking soda
3 tablespoons lemon instant pudding mix
1 (6-ounce) can frozen lemonade concentrate, thawed
1 1/4 cups buttermilk
2 eggs
1 cup shredded coconut

The glaze:
8 ounces cream cheese, softened
2 cups confectioners' sugar
1/2 cup (1 stick) margarine, softened
1 teaspoon vanilla extract

For the cake, combine the flour, sugar, baking soda, pudding mix, lemonade concentrate, buttermilk and eggs in a mixing bowl. Beat for 4 minutes or until smooth and creamy. Stir in the coconut. Pour into a greased and floured 9×13-inch cake pan. Bake at 350 degrees for 45 minutes.

For the glaze, combine the cream cheese, confectioners' sugar, margarine and vanilla in a food processor and process until smooth. Pour over the hot cake. Cool completely before serving. Store in the refrigerator or freezer. Garnish with additional coconut.

Makes 15 servings

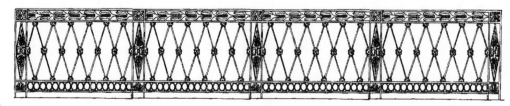

plum cake

The cake:
2 cups sifted self-rising flour, sifted again
2 cups sugar
1 cup vegetable oil
3 eggs
2 small jars baby food strained plums
1 teaspoon ground cinnamon
1 teaspoon ground cloves

The glaze:
1 cup confectioners' sugar
2 tablespoons (about) milk
1/2 teaspoon vanilla extract

For the cake, combine the flour, sugar, oil, eggs, plums, cinnamon and cloves in a mixing bowl and mix well. Pour into a greased and floured bundt pan or tube pan. Bake at 350 degrees for 45 to 50 minutes or until the cake tests done.

For the glaze, combine the confectioners' sugar, milk and vanilla in a bowl, adding more or less milk to reach the desired consistency. Pour over the warm cake.

Makes 16 servings

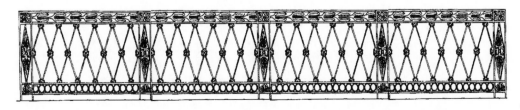

Pound Cake Squares

1 package pound cake mix
2 eggs
1/2 cup (1 stick) butter, softened
1 (1-pound) package confectioners' sugar
8 ounces cream cheese, softened
2 eggs
1 teaspoon vanilla extract
1/2 cup chopped pecans (optional)

Combine the cake mix, 2 eggs and the butter in a mixing bowl and beat until smooth. Spread in a greased 9×13-inch cake pan. Place the confectioners' sugar in a bowl, reserving 3 tablespoons for the topping. Add the cream cheese, 2 eggs and the vanilla and beat until smooth. Stir in the pecans. Spread over the cake mix layer. Bake at 350 degrees for 45 minutes. Sprinkle the reserved confectioners' sugar over the warm cake. Cut into squares.

Makes 15 servings

Note: These squares make a great alternative to brownies. They're delicious for any event, from teas to tailgating.

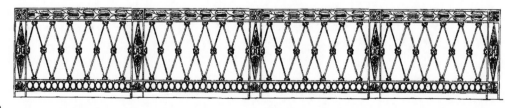

Praline Cake

1 package yellow cake mix
1/2 cup (1 stick) butter
1 (1-pound) package light brown sugar
2 tablespoons all-purpose flour
2 eggs, beaten
1 teaspoon vanilla extract
1 1/2 cups coarsely chopped pecans

Prepare the cake mix using the package directions. Pour into 2 greased and floured 9×13-inch cake pans. Bake at 350 degrees for 25 to 30 minutes or until the cakes test done. Cool on a wire rack. Melt the butter in a large skillet, Whisk the brown sugar, flour and eggs together in a bowl and stir into the butter. Bring to a boil. Reduce the heat to low. Cook for 3 minutes. Stir in the vanilla and pecans. Spread evenly over the cooled cakes. Bake at 400 degrees for 8 minutes to set the topping. Cool completely. Cut into strips.

Makes about 64 strips

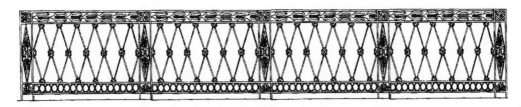

Microwave Peanut Toffee

$^1/_2$ cup finely chopped unsalted peanuts
$^1/_2$ cup (1 stick) butter or margarine
1 cup sugar
$^1/_4$ cup water
1 cup peanut butter and milk chocolate candy morsels
$^1/_4$ cup finely chopped unsalted peanuts

Spread $^1/_2$ cup peanuts in a 9-inch circle on a greased baking sheet or on a foil-lined baking sheet coated with nonstick cooking spray. Coat the top 2 inches of a 2$^1/_2$-quart glass bowl with some of the butter. Place the remaining butter in the bowl. Add the sugar and water without stirring. Microwave on High for 8 minutes or until the mixture just begins to turn a light brown. Pour over the peanuts on the baking sheet. Sprinkle with the candy morsels. Let stand for 1 minute. Spread the melted candy evenly over the peanut mixture. Sprinkle with $^1/_4$ cup peanuts. Chill until firm. Break into bite-size pieces. Store in an airtight container.

Makes 1 pound

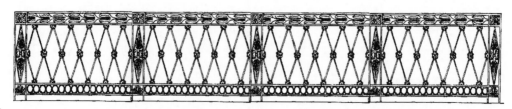

chocolate caramel crackers

1 sleeve unsalted saltine crackers
1 cup (2 sticks) butter or margarine
1 cup packed brown sugar
12 ounces miniature milk chocolate chips
1/2 cup chopped nuts (optional)

Arrange saltine crackers in a single layer in a 10×15-inch baking pan lined with heavy-duty foil and sprayed with nonstick cooking spray. Melt the butter in a saucepan over medium heat. Stir in the brown sugar. Bring to a boil. Boil gently for 3 minutes. Pour over the crackers. Bake at 300 degrees for 20 minutes. Sprinkle evenly with the chocolate chips. Let stand for 1 minute. Spread the melted chocolate evenly over the crackers. Sprinkle with the nuts. Chill, covered, until firm. Break into bite-size pieces.

Makes 15 to 20 servings

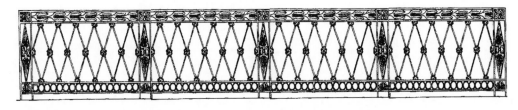

Peanut Butter Balls

1 (1-pound) package confectioners' sugar
1 cup (2 sticks) butter, softened
1 (12-ounce) jar crunchy peanut butter
1 package chocolate almond bark

Cream the confectioners' sugar and butter in a bowl. Add the peanut butter and mix well. Shape into balls. Melt the almond bark in a double boiler. Dip the peanut butter balls into the melted bark using a heavy plastic spoon and place on waxed paper until firm.

Makes about 5 dozen medium-size balls

Note: Double or triple the recipe to have enough for gift giving and for yourself at holiday time. Pack them in festive containers for friends.

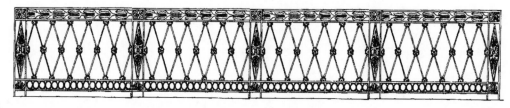

Clue Cookies

6 cups frosted corn flakes
1 cup sugar
1 cup light corn syrup
1 cup peanut butter

Measure the frosted corn flakes into a large mixing bowl. Combine the sugar and corn syrup in a saucepan. Bring to a boil, stirring constantly to prevent burning. Add the peanut butter and stir until melted and smooth. Pour over the corn flakes and stir gently to combine. Spread evenly on a baking sheet lined with foil and sprayed with nonstick cooking spray. Let cool. Break into bite-size pieces. Store in a sealable plastic bag.

Makes 20 servings

Note: Kids love this, not to mention husbands. As soon as you stir up a batch, they will appear immediately.

New England Squares

2 cups graham cracker crumbs
1 1/3 cups prepared mincemeat
1 1/3 cups sweetened condensed milk

Combine the graham cracker crumbs and mincemeat in a mixing bowl. Stir in the condensed milk and mix well. Spoon into a well-greased 9x13-inch cake pan. Bake at 350 degrees for 30 minutes or until light brown. Cool in the pan. Cut into squares.

Makes 12 servings

Note: Try making these easy and tasty treats in the fall.

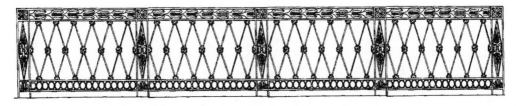

Southern Chocolate Mint Brownies

4 eggs
2 cups sugar
1 cup all-purpose flour
1 cup baking cocoa
1 cup (2 sticks) butter or
  margarine, melted

1 teaspoon vanilla extract
1/2 teaspoon peppermint extract
Mint Cream Frosting (below)
3 ounces unsweetened chocolate
3 tablespoons butter or margarine

Beat the eggs lightly with a wire whisk in a large mixing bowl. Whisk in the sugar. Combine the flour and baking cocoa. Stir into the egg mixture. Stir in 1 cup butter, the vanilla and peppermint extract. Pour into a greased 10×15-inch baking pan. Bake at 350 degrees for 15 to 18 minutes or until a wooden pick inserted in the center comes out clean. Cool in the pan on a wire rack. Spread Mint Cream Frosting over the brownie layer. Freeze for 15 minutes. Melt the chocolate with 3 tablespoons butter in a heavy saucepan over low heat, stirring constantly. Spread over the frosting using a pastry brush. Chill until firm. Cut into squares. Store in the refrigerator.

Makes about 2 dozen

Mint Cream Frosting

1/4 cup (1/2 stick) butter or
  margarine, softened
2 3/4 cups sifted confectioners' sugar

2 to 3 tablespoons milk
1/2 teaspoon peppermint extract
3 or 4 drops green food coloring

Cream the butter in a mixing bowl at medium speed. Add the confectioners' sugar gradually, beating well after each addition. Add enough milk to make of a spreading consistency. Stir in the peppermint extract and food coloring.

Makes 2 cups

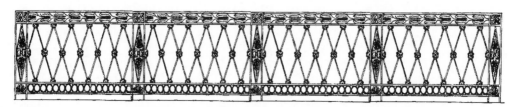

Blonde Brownies

1/2 cup (1 stick) margarine
2 cups packed brown sugar
2 eggs
2 teaspoons vanilla extract
1 cup sifted all-purpose flour, sifted again
2 teaspoons baking powder
1 teaspoon salt
1/2 cup chopped pecans
1 cup flaked coconut

Melt the margarine with the brown sugar in a saucepan over medium heat, stirring constantly until smooth. Remove from the heat and cool slightly. Beat in the eggs and vanilla. Add the flour, baking powder and salt and mix well. Stir in the pecans and coconut. Pour into a greased 9×12-inch baking pan. Bake at 350 degrees for 30 minutes.

Makes 32 squares

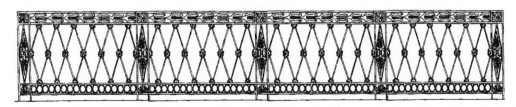

chocolate chunk cookies

1 cup (2 sticks) unsalted butter, softened
1 cup packed light brown sugar
1/2 cup granulated sugar
2 teaspoons vanilla extract
2 extra-large eggs, at room temperature
2 cups all-purpose flour
1 teaspoon baking soda
1 teaspoon kosher salt
20 ounces semisweet chocolate chunks

Cream the butter, brown sugar and granulated sugar in a mixing bowl until light and fluffy. Stir in the vanilla. Add the eggs 1 at a time and mix well. Sift the flour, baking soda and salt together. Add to the creamed mixture. Beat on low speed just until mixed. Fold in the chocolate chunks. Drop by rounded tablespoonfuls (or use a 1 3/4-inch ice cream scoop) onto a baking parchment-lined cookie sheet. Flatten slightly with a dampened hand. Bake at 350 degrees for 15 minutes. Cool slightly on the cookie sheet. Remove to a wire rack to cool completely.

Makes 36 to 40

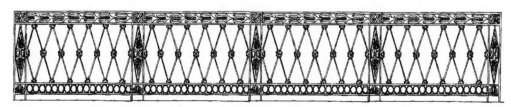

Brickle Cookies

1 package butter-recipe cake mix
1 egg, beaten
2/3 cup vegetable oil
1 package toffee bits

Combine the cake mix, egg, oil and toffee bits in a bowl and mix well. Shape into 1-inch balls. Place 2 inches apart on a cookie sheet. Bake at 350 degrees for 10 minutes.

Makes 5 dozen

Nut Cookies

2/3 cup butter, softened
1 1/2 cups packed brown sugar
2 eggs
2 1/2 cups all-purpose flour
1 teaspoon baking soda
1 teaspoon ground cinnamon
1/4 teaspoon ground cloves
1/4 teaspoon salt
2 cups chopped nuts

Cream the butter and brown sugar in a mixing bowl until light and fluffy. Add the eggs and mix well. Combine the flour, baking soda, cinnamon, cloves and salt in a bowl. Add to the creamed mixture and mix well. Stir in the nuts. Drop by rounded tablespoonfuls 2 inches apart onto a greased cookie sheet. Bake at 350 degrees until brown.

Makes about 4 dozen

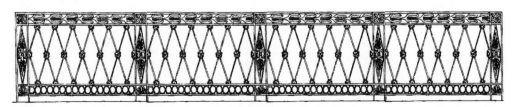

Buttermilk Pie

1 1/2 cups sugar
1/4 cup all-purpose flour
1/2 cup (1 stick) butter, melted
1/2 cup nonfat buttermilk
3 eggs, beaten
1/2 teaspoon vanilla extract
1 unbaked (9-inch) pie shell

Stir the sugar and flour together in a mixing bowl. Add the butter, buttermilk, eggs and vanilla and mix well. Pour into the pie shell. Bake at 350 degrees for 50 to 60 minutes or until the top is golden brown and a knife inserted in the center comes out clean.

Makes 6 to 8 servings

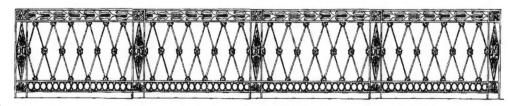

chocolate chess pie

1 1/2 cups sugar
1/2 cup (1 stick) margarine, melted
1 (5-ounce) can evaporated milk
2 eggs, beaten
3 1/2 tablespoons baking cocoa
1 teaspoon vanilla extract
1 unbaked (9-inch) pie shell

Combine the sugar, margarine, evaporated milk, eggs, baking cocoa and vanilla in a bowl and mix well. Pour into the pie shell. Bake at 325 degrees for 40 to 45 minutes.

Makes 6 to 8 servings

Note: Bake the filling in small tart shells, if desired. The filling will make about 11 tarts. Baking time will be 30 to 35 minutes. This is a great dessert for unexpected company.

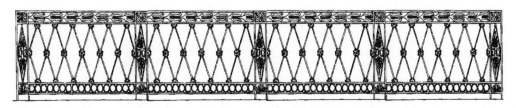

chocolate Mousse pie

8 ounces cream cheese, softened
1 cup heavy cream or whipping cream
2 (4-ounce) packages chocolate instant pudding mix
2 cups milk
1/2 cup sugar
1/4 cup Kahlúa, or 1 teaspoon peppermint extract
1 teaspoon vanilla extract
1 large graham cracker pie shell
1 chocolate bar, shaved

Combine the cream cheese, whipping cream, pudding mix, milk, sugar, Kahlúa and vanilla in a large mixing bowl. Beat at high speed until thick and fluffy. Pour into the pie shell. Sprinkle with the shaved chocolate. Chill for at least 2 hours.

Makes 8 servings

Note: Use a dark or milk chocolate bar for the topping, if desired. This dessert is wonderful at Christmas when you substitute the peppermint extract for the Kahlúa.

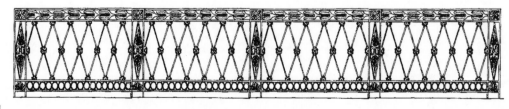

Very Easy Chocolate Pie

1 package fudge brownie mix
1 (4-ounce) package chocolate instant pudding mix
1 cup milk
1 pint vanilla ice cream, softened
Whipped topping

Prepare the brownie mix using the package directions for an 8×8-inch pan.
Spread the batter into a 10-inch pie plate. Bake at 350 degrees until done.
Cool on a wire rack. Combine the pudding mix and milk in a bowl and mix
well. Fold in the ice cream. Pour into the brownie pie shell. Freeze until firm.
Let stand at room temperature for 15 minutes before serving. Top with
whipped topping.

Makes 8 servings

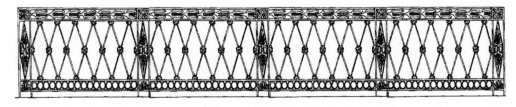

Harvest Moon Pie

4 cups thinly sliced peeled apples
1 heaping cup cranberries
1 cup packed dried apricots, cut into small pieces
1 1/4 cups sugar
2 tablespoons all-purpose flour
1/2 teaspoon ground cinnamon
1/4 teaspoon nutmeg
1/4 teaspoon salt
1 (2-crust) pie pastry
Butter

Combine the apples, cranberries and dried apricots in a large bowl.
Combine the sugar, flour, cinnamon, nutmeg and salt in a bowl and mix
well. Add to the fruit mixture and toss to combine. Pour the filling into a 9-inch
pie plate lined with one of the pie pastries. Dot with butter. Top with the
remaining pastry, sealing the edge and cutting vents. Bake at 425 degrees
for 40 to 50 minutes or until golden brown.

Makes 8 servings

Note: Try serving this pie along with your traditional pumpkin pie on Thanksgiving.

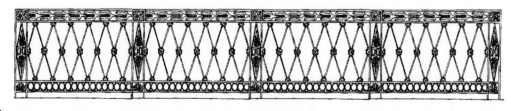

Peacharoon Freezer Pie

4 cups sliced peeled fresh peaches
1 cup sugar
1/4 teaspoon almond extract
1 1/2 cups macaroon crumbs
1 cup heavy cream or whipping cream

Mash the peaches in a bowl or purée them in a blender or food processor. Combine the puréed peaches, sugar and almond extract in a bowl. Chill while preparing the crust. Press the cookie crumbs over the bottom and up the side of an 8-inch cake pan, reserving 1/4 cup crumbs for the topping. Whip the cream in a mixing bowl until stiff peaks form. Fold into the peach mixture. Pour into the crumb crust. Sprinkle the reserved cookie crumbs over the top. Freeze, covered with foil. Let stand at room temperature for about 20 minutes before serving.

Makes 8 to 10 servings

Note: Make this dessert in the summertime when fresh peaches are in season. It's great to have on hand in the freezer. Try freezing some in individual serving dishes as well.

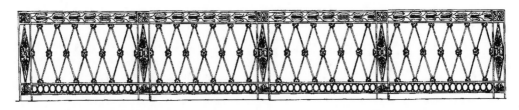

Honey Bourbon Pecan Pie

1/4 cup (1/2 stick) unsalted butter, softened
1 cup sugar
4 eggs
1/2 cup light corn syrup
1/4 cup honey
1 1/4 cups (or more) pecan halves
1 tablespoon bourbon
2 teaspoons vanilla extract
1 unbaked (9-inch) pie shell

Cream the butter and sugar in a large bowl until light and fluffy. Beat in the eggs all at once. Stir in the corn syrup and honey. Add the pecans, bourbon and vanilla and mix well. Pour into the pie shell. Bake at 400 degrees for 5 minutes. Reduce the temperature to 325 degrees. Bake for 45 minutes or until done.

Makes 8 servings

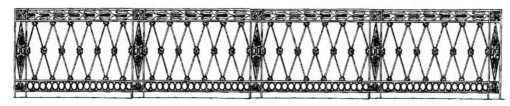

Favorite Pecan Pie

1/2 cup (1 stick) butter
1 cup light corn syrup
1 cup sugar
4 eggs
1 1/2 teaspoons vanilla extract
1/2 to 3/4 teaspoon salt, or to taste
1 cup (or more) whole pecans or pecan pieces
1 unbaked (10-inch) deep-dish pie shell

Melt the butter in a saucepan over low heat. Add the corn syrup and sugar. Cook over low heat until the sugar is dissolved and the mixture looks glossy. Remove from the heat and let cool for a few minutes. Beat the eggs, vanilla and salt together in a bowl. Add the warm corn syrup mixture gradually to the egg mixture, beating until smooth. Place the pecans in the pie shell and pour the filling over the top. Bake at 325 degrees for 55 to 60 minutes or until done.

Makes 8 servings

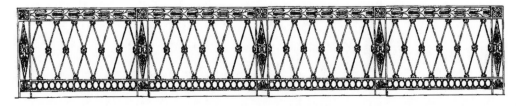

Lemon Tart

The crust:
2 cups all-purpose flour
$^1/_4$ cup confectioners' sugar
$^1/_4$ teaspoon salt
$^1/_2$ cup (1 stick) butter, cut into pieces
$^1/_4$ cup lard
1 egg yolk
1 tablespoon apple cider vinegar
1 teaspoon vanilla extract
1 teaspoon lemon juice

The filling:
4 eggs, beaten
$1^1/_3$ cups sugar
$^2/_3$ cup fresh lemon juice
$^1/_3$ cup milk
3 tablespoons all-purpose flour
2 teaspoons grated lemon zest
$^1/_8$ teaspoon salt

For the crust, combine the flour, confectioners' sugar and salt in a food processor and pulse to combine. Add the butter and lard and process until crumbly. Combine the egg yolk, vinegar, vanilla and lemon juice in a small bowl and mix well. Add to the processor bowl and process just until combined. Shape into a ball. Chill, wrapped in plastic wrap, for 30 minutes. Roll out on a lightly floured surface and fit into a tart pan. Bake at 350 degrees until set and golden brown.

For the filling, whisk the eggs and sugar together in a bowl. Add the lemon juice, milk, flour, lemon zest and salt and mix well. Pour into the tart crust. Bake at 325 degrees for 25 minutes or until set. Garnish with whipped cream, fresh raspberries and mint leaves.

Makes 8 servings

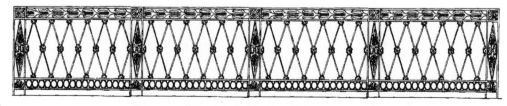

Index

Raising the Torch!

A Salute to Birmingham's Southern Cuisine

Jefferson County Medical Society Alliance
901 South 18th Street
Birmingham, Alabama 35205
205-933-8601

YOUR ORDER	QTY	@	TOTAL
Raising the Torch! at $22.95 per book		22.95	$
Alabama residents add $1.84 sales tax per book		1.84	$
Postage and handling at $4.00 per shipment			$
		TOTAL	$

Make check payable to
Jefferson County Medical Society Alliance

Name

Street Address

City   State   Zip

Telephone

Photocopies will be accepted.

176